The "I AM" Solution ™

Simple Practices to Transform FEAR Back to LOVE

Dr. Karmen Smith

MSW LCSW DD

Copyright © 2016 Dr. Karmen Smith

Dr. Karmen Smith, MSW LCSW DD
Karlcsw@gmail.com
www.DrKarmen.com

All rights reserved. This book or any portion thereof may not be reproduced or used in any manner whatsoever without the express written permission of the publisher except for the use of brief quotations in a book review.

Printed in the United States of America
ISBN: 978-0-9971205-0-9

Publisher:
NSITEFUL

PO BOX 92243
Henderson NV 89014

Copyright © 2016 Dr. Karmen Smith

All rights reserved.

ISBN: 978-0-9971205-0-9

Disclaimer

The "I AM" Solution™ is a resource and is not intended to be a substitute for therapy or professional advice. While all attempts have been made to verify information provided in this book, neither the author nor the publisher assumes any responsibility for errors, omissions or contrary interpretation of the self-help subject matter herein. There is no guarantee of validity of accuracy of any self-help content. Any perceived slight of specific people or organizations is unintentional. The contents are solely the opinion of the author and should not be considered as a diagnosis or treatment of any kind whether medical condition or mental health disorder. If expert advice or counseling is needed, services of a competent professional should be sought. The author and publisher assume no responsibility or liability and specifically disclaim any warranty, express or implied, for any products or services mentioned, or any techniques or practices described. The purchaser or reader of this book assumes responsibility for the use of these self-help materials and information.

DEDICATION

I dedicate this book to my parents, Ralph and Kanzetta Harris, who used their challenges, fear and suffering as a way to be of service to many. Thank you, for showing me that the path to helping others is littered with our own transformational debris.

ACKNOWLEDGMENTS

I would like to acknowledge all the people in my life who caused me to grow spiritually by pushing my buttons. I'm awake to the fact that without challenges I would not be able to develop the areas in my identity that needed spiritual definition. I would like to acknowledge my colleagues at The Department of Family Services Clinical Unit. They're brilliant and compassionate and I'm honored to work with them. I would like to acknowledge all those people I used to think were my enemy but were actually my shamans in disguise. They helped me take their costume off and recognize them for who they were: my projection of wounds that needed healing. Thank you to my editor Andrea of WritersWay who has been patient and detailed. My mentor Dr. Paul Leon Masters. Thank you to my enlightenment circle, empaths unite group, my friends who I can count on one hand, my two supportive sisters and son, Lauren, who has been one of my biggest spiritual teachers. Thank you to the Creator who made me who "I AM."

Thank you
Dr. Karmen Smith

TABLE OF CONTENTS

INTRODUCTION 1
CHAPTER ONE I AM THAT I AM 12
CHAPTER TWO FEAR LEADS TO SUFFERING 16
CHAPTER THREE WHAT IS TRAUMA? 29
CHAPTER FOUR THE HUMAN HAMSTER WHEEL 44
CHAPTER FIVE F.E.A.R. = FROM EGO ALTERING REALITY 62
CHAPTER SIX POWER AND CONTROL REACTIONS (PCR) 89
CHAPTER SEVEN FORGIVENESS 101
CHAPTER EIGHT THE CONNECTION 117
CHAPTER NINE THE FIVE POINTED STAR 125
CHAPTER TEN PRACTICE LOVE 138
CHAPTER ELEVEN PRACTICE COMPASSION 150
CHAPTER TWELVE PRACTICE GRATITUDE 156
CHAPTER THIRTEEN PRACTICE ACCEPTANCE 168
CHAPTER FOURTEEN PRACTICE TRUST 182
CHAPTER FIFTEEN THE "I AM" SOLUTION 193
ABOUT THE AUTHOR 204

MY FAVORITE QUOTE

"Our deepest fear is not that we are inadequate. Our deepest fear is that we are powerful beyond measure. It is our light, not our darkness that most frightens us. We ask ourselves, Who am I to be brilliant, gorgeous, talented, fabulous? Actually, who are you not to be? You are a child of God. Your playing small does not serve the world. There is nothing enlightened about shrinking so that other people won't feel insecure around you. We are all meant to shine, as children do. We were born to make manifest the glory of God that is within us. It's not just in some of us; it's in everyone. And as we let our own light shine, we unconsciously give other people permission to do the same. As we are liberated from our own fear, our presence automatically liberates others."

This inspiring quote by Marianne Williamson is from her book, <u>A Return To Love: Reflections on the Principles of A Course in Miracles</u>.

CHAPTER VIDEO'S

Each chapter has a video that goes into detail about the items discussed in each section. The videos are short and included to enhance the experience of The "I AM" SOLUTION TM.
There are 19+ video's included in the series and all can be viewed at DRKARMEN.COM then click on the tab *Chapter video's*. Enjoy this added bonus which is my way to connect with you during the process of enlightenment.

Peace and Blessings
Dr. Karmen

INTRODUCTION

"In the Heart of all things, of whatever there is in the Universe, dwells the Lord."
~ Upanishads

"My client was sent to the hospital because her boyfriend knocked her unconscious. Bless his heart." You may not have heard this quote before because this was from my mother who was a social worker. I had the benefit of growing up listening to some of the stories she would tell about her work experiences. I was about 14 when she made this statement and I didn't appreciate the "wisdom" behind her words. I've forgotten many of the stories she conveyed but I do remember this particular quote because it confused me.

I recall correcting her and saying, "You mean, 'Bless *her* heart.' "A child doesn't say, When I grow up I want to hurt the ones I love the most," she explained. "That's never the goal of any child. This man's girlfriend is in the hospital and getting positive attention and services will be provided for her. Yet both of them are suffering. If I'm going to help him, I need to see him the way God sees him…with compassion. I need to replace the way he sees himself and it starts with a blessing."

My mother understood that only when he could be how she saw him—as his true self— could change take place. My mother summed up her philosophy, spirituality and the art of social work in that one example. I was fortunate that she shared it with her 14-year-old daughter even though I didn't understand it at the time. I'm grateful because as I've come to a deeper understanding about her view of the world I can see the infinite truth it holds.

My mother had a tremendous influence on me, so you may think my first career choice would have been social work. However, a career in social work wasn't even in my conscious awareness. In high school I won several awards including the state championship for dramatic and prose interpretation. I had taken acting lessons since the age of eight. I would escape the trauma and drama of my childhood by watching television and movies.

I lived for everything that had to do with acting. I attended the American Academy of Dramatic Arts after high school graduation. In both Los Angeles and New York I auditioned and pursued work as an actress. When enough work wasn't available, I decided to pursue my other passion: psychology. I was afraid to enroll in college because of a traumatic experience in fifth grade (I discuss it later in the book). I had a tremendous fear of school and enrolling in a class in college represented a big emotional hurdle.

I took baby steps and ultimately enrolled in one class at the community college: Abnormal Psychology. I was hooked. I remember calling my mother and raving about how interesting it was and how I was hanging on every word the professor spoke. I sat in the front of the class and discovered that instead of taking notes I could just memorize his lectures. I began the journey of overcoming my fear of being stupid I had carried all my life. Every time the class covered a new topic I was excited to call home and talk about it with my mother.

On one call I talked to her about wanting my father's brain when he died. I wanted to study it for structural abnormalities. My father was a huge catalyst for my interest in psychology because our relationship felt like an emotional roller coaster. During my early childhood I felt sadness and guilt when he wasn't around and in my teen years I felt anger and rage toward him. As an adult the anger was suppressed because I lived thousands of miles away.

GROWING UP AS AN EMPATH.

I've known that I can feel another person's energy since I was little. Family gatherings were a barrage of energy fields vying for my attention. Going to the mall was my mom's idea of pleasure but to me it could be emotionally assaulting and draining. So I would refuse to go to family gatherings or shopping preferring to stay in my room where I found peace. My parents' and sisters' bedrooms had two doors creating a high energy flow. My room had one door and was in the corner of the house which I found soothing and safe.

I've learned over the years to view my sensitivity to energy as a gift rather than a curse mostly because of Dr. Judith Orloft. I miraculously ran across an article that Dr. Orloft wrote and she put a name to my accelerated empathy: empath. <u>An empath is one who's very sensitive to the energy or emotions of others and the environment.</u> When I was growing up I felt everything that was going on inside our home: my father's anger, my mother's rage and the psychological dance they played with each other. As a result I isolated myself in my room withdrawing into movies, plays and dramatic forensic competitions.

My empathic abilities were a curse at that time because I didn't have the vocabulary to describe my emotions and where they were coming from. I just knew I could not only feel things but I could not separate what was my feeling or another's emotional energy. Because my parents were angry I was angry every time I was at home. I was picking up on feelings and information even though it wasn't being verbalized.

Now this ability is a blessing in my life. When I AM whole within me it's a gift, however when I have victim thoughts it's amplified because I absorb the negative energy around me. The emotions of powerlessness and victimization affect me as if they were my own experiences of trauma. When I was growing up as an empath it felt like my father had a dark cloud of energy around him most of the time. What I was picking up on was how he viewed himself and the world.

As a teenager I rebelled against my father and developed hateful, angry feelings toward him. I didn't realize I was setting the framework for my own suffering. Today I AM grateful for having him as my father because he stimulated my curiosity about mental illness, the brain and human behavior. He was an essential compass guiding me toward my purpose as well as my spiritual development of compassion and love.

When I turned 40, and after a spiritual revelation and a calling, I became an ordained minister. As I identified with my higher source (or inner Hero) the energies of fear didn't affect my consciousness in such an all-consuming way. As an empath it was important that I find a way to process second hand and personal trauma that wouldn't perpetuate a cycle of suffering in my life. During my journey I recognized how each direction was turning me inward to self-discovery.

What if it's true that we pick our parents? If that's so, then we pick them when we're still in Spirit form based on what we need to learn about BEING THE I AM. So God or Universal Energy desires us to embrace love and forgiveness in order to be who we are. With a wall around our hearts due to fear-based thinking, we may choose a parent to abandon us and through that pain and anger we can find out what we have inside that never goes away. These parents will help bring us to a point where we love ourselves; then we can give them the love and forgiveness they need. These types of events can lead us to our knowing of and being the I AM.

LOOKING AT YOUR JOURNEY FROM A HIGHER VANTAGE POINT.

Studying acting with Stella Adler, a famous acting teacher, was a life-changing experience. She taught me how to formulate a character based on what was written in the script. The personality of the character had to be believable to me for it to come to life. I had to know what the character thought and felt, without judging their traits. I also needed to develop a past history of the character even though it may not be written in the script. All these steps were necessary to bring a role to life.

This process taught me how human behavior is created based on intention, family, environment, traumatic events and happy occasions. These life experiences can bring about love or fear-based thinking. An interesting role is one where the character transforms during the course of the script from Fear to Love. We feel compassion for them and a connection because subconsciously we know it's our journey.

Psychology gave me a framework for how thoughts and feelings come together to form our behaviors. I discovered that our behavior is based on how we see the world and our role in it. I learned that feeling anxious and unsafe will dictate the choices we make. Our choices can be based on our fear of intimacy, fear of failure or fear of not being good enough. It can also come from the security in knowing everything will be okay. When we make decisions based on our fear it can be the catalyst for positive change or perpetual chaos.

My degree in mental health research allowed me to delve deeper into the functions of the brain and why Thoughts-Feelings-Reactions (TFR) are so difficult to change. Learning how we process information helped me design a framework that explains the structure behind human behavior that causes suffering. The ego, which is fear-based thinking, can be a difficult concept to understand but the "Human Hamster Wheel of Suffering" provides a simple visual to explain how fear-based thinking can create a chaotic life. The ego can block the love we were meant to share by perpetuating fear-based thinking. When we're on The Human Hamster Wheel we experience anxiety, resentful relationships and struggle because our fear doesn't allow us to express the love within.

Spiritualty and the wisdom of the sages provided insights that the cause of the cycle of suffering is Fear. Gratitude, Acceptance, Compassion and Trust can generate LOVE. Love is who we are and knowing who we are can unlock the keys to all the gifts the Universe has to offer.

Buddha is recognized by Buddhists as an awakened or enlightened teacher who shared his insights to help sentient beings end their suffering through the elimination of ignorance and craving. Buddhism teaches the four noble truths which are:

* The truth of suffering (*dukkha*)
* The truth of the cause of suffering (*samudaya*)
* The truth of the end of suffering (*nirhodha*)
* The truth of the path that frees us from suffering (*magga*)

Put more simply: Life can be difficult but this struggle is something we build ourselves and it's possible for us to live in an ongoing experience of awakening, freedom, happiness, compassion, peace and love. And there are paths we can follow to reach this state.

Many of the major religions or paths to enlightenment address the issues of suffering which center around fear. The Bible has many passages that denounce fear in order to align with love and compassion. The Kabbalah which means "receiving" is an esoteric method, discipline and school of thought that originated in Judaism. This set of teachings explains the relationship between an unchanging, eternal and mysterious infinity (God) and the mortal and finite Universe (God's creation). Kabbalah seeks to define the nature of the Universe and the human being and the nature and purpose of existence. It also presents methods to aid understanding of the concepts and thereby attain spiritual realization or Oneness with the Creator. The Kabbalists explain that the blockage (or challenges) we all face is called Satan (Say-ton). Satan is not a person or evil deity who causes suffering; instead it's our fears that create the suffering and chaos that we can learn to overcome. The only way to overcome the challenge or fear is to be more like the light (love). Almost every spiritual tradition or practice offers a method to transform the vibrational fear energy that creates struggle back to love which manifests peace.

"*Wherever the hero may wander, whatever he may do, he is ever in the presence of his own essence for he has the perfected eye to see. There is no separateness.*

*Thus, just as the way of social participation may lead in the end to a realization of the
All in the individual, so that of exile brings the hero to the Self in all."*
~ Joseph Campbell

Mythologist Joseph Campbell was a masterful storyteller who researched the myths and stories from different cultures around the world and discovered a unifying theme. Campbell explained how challenging experiences could be seen as initiatory adventures that call forth our inner Hero. The typical adventure of the archetype known as The Hero is about the person who goes out and achieves great deeds on behalf of his group, tribe or civilization. Campbell's research showed a connection between ancient stories and the emotional concerns of modern life and how they're distinctive. The hero rises above the fear to conquer the challenge which caused the suffering. These myths are our story if only we can be awake to comprehend that we're all being called to overcome our own suffering and by telling our story of triumph we awaken others.

In this book my intention is to teach simple practices that can bring out the inner Hero by transforming Fear back to Love. The inner Hero when acknowledged and activated gives us the ability to overcome any perceived external limitations. I intend to reveal that the same way we create our suffering is the road map to expand love.

I've attended many classes and heard several motivational speeches that left me feeling inspired and elevated but the feelings were intellectual and temporary. The "I AM" Solution is a practice you can use to create and reach your highest potential by transforming Fear back to Love. I also intend to dispel the myths or lies that we're not enough. We've believed for too long that we're dependent on outside circumstances or conditions for our strength, joy, safety, abundance and power. It takes practice to live life from the internal paradigm instead of the external one.

We are not victims; we have the inner workings to manifest everything we think we are. Part of our DNA is the code to success, harmony and unity. We are the solution to any challenge we have. We can practice being the solution in any circumstance.

The exercises and practices I've provided in this book will give you opportunities to gain more light. This light can awaken your inner glow and purpose illuminating your daily journey. The practices also train your brain to think in ways that are in line with the inner Hero or God consciousness. By thinking like the Creator you defeat the victim identity which is based on fear.

The "I AM" Solution has practical applications and I use myself as the case study. In my life I've experienced the debilitating effect of fear. I was angry, resentful, controlling, critical and manipulative. What I didn't know was that those feelings stemmed from my underlying fear of not feeling safe, since I had a childhood of domestic violence and chaos. It manifested in my adult life in job and family situations. When I knew people were talking about me behind my back I panicked and went on the defensive. I attacked every time I didn't feel safe. I ultimately learned to break that cycle with the simple practices I share in this book.

I say simple practices because they sound simple on paper but they're intended to push you past your fears. The fearful ego will not want to participate and will tell you how stupid the practices are but recognize that the ego does not like change. Your challenge is to push past your fears anyway no matter how scared you are. This is the way toward more loving relationships with yourself and all beings. An abundant magical existence awaits beyond fear.

Looking back on my incredible journey it makes perfect sense: Dysfunctional family, Acting, Psychology and Spirituality all came together to increase my Oneness and knowledge of the infinite forces that desire our highest consciousness. It's been about 40 years since my mother explained "Who We Are" and The "I AM" Solution is based on her sacred truth.

Remember you have everything you need within you to transform Fear back to Love.

Dr. Karmen Smith, LCSW DD

Reference

When we look back on our life from a higher vantage point, we can see the direction and turns we took as having a purpose. Every turn had a meaning and every challenge a reward. My upbringing was a blessing and what I thought were setbacks were setting me up for something bigger than I could imagine.

In this video I look at the twists and turns that have happened in my life and I can see the perfect plan unfold.

Video, "Using Your Imagination to Create" at drkarmen.com

CHAPTER ONE

I AM THAT I AM

*"This is my Bible, I am what it says I am, I have what it says I have,
I can do what it says I can do."*
~ Joel Olsten

In the Bible there's a name for God which was revealed in the story of Moses. When Moses saw the burning bush it wasn't being consumed and he went closer to investigate the light. He approached the strange phenomenon and was told to take off his shoes because he was standing on holy ground. Moses complied with the request and was asked to pick up a snake by the tail.

When I first read this passage I was struck by the fact that Moses was told by God to pick up a venomous snake by the wrong end. We all know that to handle poisonous snakes the head and jaws need to be secured so it won't bite. The voice of God told Moses to pick up the snake by the tail which sounds like suicide. Moses did what was asked of him by putting his fear aside for greater knowledge. In that fearless moment he was able to recognize he was in the presence of Divine energy that could light a bush without consuming it. Moses, with that presence, wasn't afraid for his safety. His attention was on the power that provided peace and vitality. He wanted to experience that presence and be it.

The powerful presence told him to go to Egypt and tell Pharaoh to let his people go. Moses asked, "Whom should I say sent me?" And God said, "I AM that I AM".

THE "I AM" SOLUTION™

When Moses was asked to take off his shoes because he was on holy ground he was being tested. He displayed a childlike awe and curiosity. When he picked up the snake he showed courage. God called him for a mission. When Moses asked, "Whom should I say sent me?" God knew Moses and Moses recognized God. The same attributes were in both therefore there was no separation. God said, "I AM that I AM". In other words all that Moses had cultivated within himself was matching the identity of God. He had within him everything he needed to fulfill his destiny and purpose. Moses and God became One connected and bound by the same creative consciousness they both possessed. Moses was The "I AM" Solution. He would have the light going forward. The "I AM" Solution is when everything we need is who we already are.

The "I AM" Solution is illustrated perfectly in the story of Moses. If Moses didn't see himself in that divine moment he would not have done what was needed for the exodus. If the Kingdom of God was not within him he would not have recognized God. In order for him to be the One he had to release any conditioned thought that generated the lessor frequency of fear. Sprit recognizes Spirit therefore Moses knew the identity of the One who called him to a seemingly impossible purpose.

The ultimate meaning to the challenges in our life is to move beyond Fear back to Love so we can be of service to all. The "I AM" Solution provides a framework to transform our fearful ego into the attributes of The I AM. All those attributes are within you but are covered by your fear of not being good enough or not being ready for greatness. We all have our individual hero's journey filled with challenges as well as victories. My framework includes two visuals I created of The "I AM" Solution: The Human Hamster Wheel which describes how our fear generates chaos and a Five Pointed Star that transforms us from Fear back to Love.

As we practice being the light we let the attributes of God define us. We begin to recognize God everywhere. When we're in the moment and not reacting to our ego we're primed for our purpose. While in that stillness of non-reactivity we recognize the will of God unfolding as our intentions. We are then on the path to being who we truly are. That is The "I AM" SOLUTION.

Exercise One

I would recommend getting an I AM journal to keep track of your thoughts and to process the topics that will be addressed in this book. The I AM journal can document your transformation journey and reveal the challenges that may arise. In your journal write down your thoughts about the name of God. What names do you call God and does it make you uncomfortable to think that your goal is to be more God like? Is it possible to become the qualities of God?

Reference

The solution for every challenge is to be found in who and what we truly are. Our identity is crucial in how we move through our lives. We can encounter situations as a victim or as the victor but it's up to us to determine that. Our identity choice will dictate the outcome and how we see it. The "I AM" Solution is about transforming our Fear back to Love, which is our true identity.

In this video I explain the meaning behind The "I AM" Solution. Video, "The 'I AM' Solution" at drkarmen.com

CHAPTER TWO

FEAR LEADS TO SUFFERING

"No one saves us but ourselves. No one can and no one may. We ourselves must walk the path."
~ Buddha

The police came into my bedroom and told me I had five minutes to vacate my 6,000 square foot home. One of the officers showed me a copy of a restraining order that was filed by my husband. My heart sank but I didn't have the option to fall apart. The first thing I grabbed was our four- month-old son. I took diapers and formula and stuffed a garbage bag full of clothing. I was stopped by one of the police officers and told I would need to go to court to get more items out of our house and I needed to leave now.

That was the last time I would see the items that were handed down by my mother and grandmother both of whom had passed. My sisters and I were given fine china, an antique salt and pepper shaker collection and a box full of old coins that my grandmother began collecting when she was a child. My house was where my sister's childhood pictures and heirlooms were stored and they were gone in that one day. These items could never be replaced or forgotten. The day I was forced to leave my home was the last day those items existed in my family.

The officers had little sympathy for me as I struggled to gather essentials while they followed me around the house. The police were enforcing a restraining order they thought was valid. They believed the Temporary Protective Order (TPO) was based on truth—that I was aggressive. That's probably why when I tried to pack the baby scissors for my son's fingernails the officer told me I couldn't take them. My husband also stood by supervising the forced exodus.

It was the Friday before Memorial Day weekend. An hour earlier, before the police showed up, the phone had rung; it was a man asking for my husband. I used the intercom to tell him he had a phone call. I was in the master bedroom and he was outside by the pool. I pretended to hang up but listened as a woman came on the line and they began talking. He told her, "My wife will be gone before the weekend." When I heard that I broke into the conversation by asserting, "I'm not going anywhere!" They became upset and screamed at me to hang up. I was called all sorts of names as I asserted my stance. "I'm not going anywhere; this is my home!" The next thing I knew the police were escorting me and my 4-month-old out of the majestic double doors of our dream house.

SEVEN MONTHS EARLIER.

My husband and I had just moved to a new unfamiliar city. We bought a vacant lot in a gated community to build our dream home—built to our specifications by an exceptional builder in Las Vegas. The real estate was cheaper there than in Los Angeles which is where we had been living for six years. Our imagination flourished as we included all the amenities we wanted: a pool, a Jacuzzi, a bathroom by the pool, a portacohe, an intercom system, a large media room and a view of the strip from every room in the house.

Soon after we moved into our house, my husband's secret affairs were revealed to me. I was devastated. I thought I knew him and had been very secure in our relationship. When I learned the truth, it felt like I was knocked to the ground and the floor I'd been standing on crumbled. My world which was built on my relationship and everything it held for the future fell apart. I began to question everything and nothing made sense anymore.

I was told by my husband's best friend's wife that he had been seeing many women and one woman he regularly visited in Los Angeles. Those business trips or times he was checking on his mother were rendezvous with several women. When I confronted my husband the night I found out, he admitted it. At the time I was seven months pregnant and I screamed and cried because I was afraid. I didn't know the next move and couldn't figure out what I was going to do. I felt helpless, angry, betrayed, confused and unloved. I was scared of being a single parent, on my own and I felt lost.

The more I felt like a victim, the more I needed to make him the villain. I thought I had ample ammunition just like I had against my father, another man I believed I had reason to hate. In my darkest moment I thought about ending my life. I envisioned an arrow going into my stomach killing the baby and me. I didn't have an arrow but I did have a pool. I thought the action I would take would be to drown myself, which wouldn't be hard since I couldn't swim. I couldn't stop ruminating over how my husband would feel knowing that his actions caused our death. I thought about how bad he would feel at the funeral. I believed this action would get me the result I wanted—having him feel as devastated as I felt.

As the police escorted me out, I thought about the credit and debit cards not activating at the checkout line a few days earlier; my husband had explained it away as a banking glitch. Penniless and homeless, I had no answers for what to do next. One of the officers told me I needed to go before a judge. I said I just needed to call my family so I could get a plane ticket home to Kansas City, Missouri. I had actually filed for divorce a week earlier and the officer advised me I would be charged with kidnapping if I left the state. I almost fell over. He explained I couldn't take a minor child out of Nevada without a custody agreement which once again entailed going to court. Even though I wanted to be with my family, I was told leaving would be a criminal act.

That night, and for the next three months, I slept on a cot with my infant son in a homeless shelter. I was keenly aware that my husband slept in our newly built 6,000 square foot home in a gated community with another woman. My name was still on the deed but due to the restraining order I couldn't come within 500 feet of the residence or I could be arrested. I couldn't leave the state of Nevada to be with family or I could be arrested for kidnapping.

FEAR-BASED THINKING

Fear is having a distressing emotion aroused by impending danger, evil or pain whether the threat is real or imagined. **I was afraid.** Fear can instigate the cycle of suffering and create the energy of anger, rage, shame, guilt, anxiety and depression. Fear is always the first emotion that stems from the victim trauma paradigm or what I like to call The Human Hamster Wheel of Suffering.

Many people in my profession can speak academically about the effects of trauma on others but I've painted a picture of the trauma I personally experienced. I lived through these traumatizing situations and I'm prospering now because of it (I'll explain during the course of the book how you can do the same). When I was homeless and penniless living a trauma/drama filled life, it felt as if my world had crumbled—and it had. I was in a nightmare and I couldn't wake up. I felt terrified, numb and helpless when I realized I had nowhere to go and could be living in my car with my infant son.

There were more traumatic events to come that felt as if they were intended to destroy me. My fear of being destroyed brought out anger and my ego wanted revenge for the malicious acts I felt were being done to me. My husband and I both got caught up in a cycle of "you hurt me and I'll hurt you back". Fear-based thinking led to feelings of anger, rage and sadness, which further justified manipulations, lying and acts of revenge. This pattern was the start of a perpetuated cycle of suffering which I developed as The Human Hamster Wheel of Suffering.

The Human Hamster Wheel is based on fear therefore it creates chaos. I also discovered the end of fear-based thinking which is called the Five Pointed Star. Our true identity is light because our Creator is light. When we're fearful we lose sight of our birthright and true identity. Instead of shining the light of love and giving, when in fear we spread darkness. By practicing the attributes of the Five Pointed Star we can break the cycle of fear-based thinking.

TRUST EVERYTHING IS GOING TO BE OKAY

Something miraculous happened when I was at my lowest point. As I've said, when I was told of the affairs my husband was having, I was suicidal and seven months pregnant. I looked up mental health emergencies and found a facility where I could get some help. I drove to the State Mental Health Hospital and told them I was pregnant and found out my husband was cheating—and I wanted to end it all.

The staff checked me in. I hadn't eaten all day. I sat in the middle of the quad with the TV on. I didn't know what to do. I was afraid and felt powerless and victimized. When I went to my room I couldn't sleep. It was a small room with cinder block walls, a small dresser and a single twin bed with a thin mattress on a wire frame. The staff was nice but busy and detached. At 9 pm they called for "lights out". My door was closed and through the bottom crack the light streamed through illuminating parts of the room. When my eyes adjusted I remember crying and wondering: What am I going to do?

I don't know how long I asked that question but what happened next gives me goose bumps, over 20 years later. I saw what I can only describe as gas vapors rising and swirling near the foot of my bed, near the dresser. A calming peaceful feeling came over me. I knew I was safe. I then heard a voice say, "Everything is going to be okay." I basked in that feeling of knowing everything was going to be okay. The visible gas vapor image faded but the feeling remained. I sat in the dark knowing an unseen force knew everything that was happening and everything that was going to happen. I felt safe. I could hear that voice from memory saying, "Everything is going to be okay." It was a soft, calm, peaceful voice and I instantly trusted the feeling of hope and security. I was instilled with a knowing that the Universe had my back. I wasn't alone. Instead of the fearful thoughts surrounding my future I knew everything was going to work out for my highest good. I felt secure, loved, valued and guided.

I emerged the next morning from my room asking if I could have my clothes as I was ready to leave. I told the doctor that the end of my marriage wasn't going to be the end of me or my son. I was released with well wishes and with the intention to save my marriage with counseling.

ACCEPT THAT THINGS ARE THE WAY THEY ARE.

My husband had agreed to counseling and we had attended a couples group just before he filed the restraining order. The group sessions were held at a church in the top floor classroom. Seven couples were in attendance once a week to discuss their challenges and what they were working on to improve their marriage. The one time we attended, my husband and I came in separate cars because he would be coming from work and was coming from home with the baby. The couples' session began with the instructor asking each person to tell the group something that happened the previous week that was a sign things were getting better in the relationship.

We were the last couple to go and my husband announced that the problem was he was married and if he wasn't he wouldn't have a problem. He got up and left. When the door shut I was left behind in a room full of people I didn't know. I was speechless and they didn't know what to say to me. In that moment I realized there was no saving the marriage; it was over and I had to accept what I was afraid of: divorce, poverty and being a single parent. As tears streamed down my face I pushed my son's baby stroller to the door, picked it up and headed down the long flight of stairs knowing it would be just the two of us. Not knowing how it would play out or what I would say to my husband when I got home I had to trust everything was going to be okay.

There were moments of clarity in the midst of the stressful moments when I had to affirm that God, the energy that came to me in my darkest moment, had my back. There were times when I felt attacked and wanted to attack back but it would be replaced with a peace that surpassed understanding. There were times when I felt empowered and other times when I felt lost at sea without a paddle. I had moments where I could see the light in the midst of darkness and times when I was so scared I thought my heart would beat out of my chest. I would have to practice believing everything was going to be okay. I recognized that there were attributes I had that would pull me through when the situation could have pulled me under. I had no idea at the time that what I was learning from what was happening to me I would later develop into The "I AM" Solution to help others.

FIND SOMETHING TO LOVE AND BE GRATEFUL FOR EVERYTHING

The love for my son was definitely what kept me going but it was more than that. He was born with a love within him that's healing. I know now it was a reminder of the love within each of us, of the love that was always with me symbolized outwardly in my son. This universal love sustained me through that time. I was able to recognize it in my son but it was a reflection of the higher love within me revealing itself during those stressful situations.

I also had to reconcile that this love in my son was also in my husband. It was difficult but not impossible. I had to replace fear with love to rise from feeling I was the victim. To survive the trauma, love reminded me that I couldn't surrender to the feelings of fear. Although in reading about the story of my divorce you may say I was the victim but I instinctively knew it would be detrimental if I believed I was a victim. Instead I practiced being compassionate toward the police and my husband. I knew my house and husband had made me feel safe and secure. But when both were ripped from me I had an opportunity to access the power in me that's secure in any situation.

HAVE COMPASSION FOR YOURSELF AND OTHERS.

My son's love helped me to hang on even though it would have been easier to let go, to fall into my victim story and tell people about the horrible things my husband had done to me. Instead I stopped telling the story. I began to look forward to what was next. I forgave myself for all of the red flags I'd missed. I forgave myself for believing that my hero was my husband. I had compassion for myself for participating in the vengeance seeking behaviors that gave the illusion of power. I learned through this series of events that I had created situations that would lead me to change the way I thought. How else could I have learned that my hero wasn't outside of me? In order to change my limiting beliefs I had to undergo a correction which came in the form of a life changing event: divorce.

WHEN WE REPLACE FEAR WITH LOVE, WE CREATE A LIFE WITHOUT CHAOS.

The manipulations and revenge type behaviors I initiated stopped and I no longer wanted my husband to suffer an ill fate. I forgave myself for believing I was a victim. I forgave my husband and by doing so released myself from the cycle of suffering that had been generational. I didn't want to pass on the vibrational frequency of hatred and victimization to my son. I entertained thoughts of my husband doing well and being as blessed as I was. I continued to send blessings and good will to him regardless of his actions.

The trauma of the divorce transformed me into a more enlightened person. Looking back at that time in my life when I was at my most vulnerable, I found strength. I AM grateful for the experiences that led me to practice forgiveness and compassion. I was able to forgive myself for making decisions that perpetuated the suffering of all involved. And I was able to forgive my husband knowing he helped me come to the divine truths that were revealed through the trauma.

ALL CHAOS AND TRAUMA HAVE A PURPOSE

The purpose of the trauma was the lessons I needed to learn through loss. My beliefs about myself and others needed to change. I had to recognize that I AM more powerful than any situation I encounter. My inner Hero was ignited through the loss of everything I thought gave me security. The divorce was a catalyst for my true identity to be more present, revealing endless potential and possibilities. Several things pulled me through those dark days and the lessons are still coming 20 years later.

During our journey through life we're given intricate truths as we're able to recognize them. We can have a choice as to when and if we implement them in our life. I AM grateful for the ability to learn who I AM by going through the challenges.

When I found out I couldn't leave Las Vegas, I began to resent the city. What do you think I would have created by hating the very place I lived? So I had to look at Las Vegas without the victim set of eyes. I had to practice finding something to love about the city. I looked around and saw that Las Vegas was a beautiful city with the most amazing sunsets framed by mountain ranges. I felt cocooned in supportive spiritual energy and recognized the presence of God around me. In this city I found the God energy in a small cinder block room in the state hospital.

These thoughts were empowering and devalued the victim mentality that could have conquered my psyche. My intention is to practice, in each moment, to be compassionate, grateful, accepting and trusting that everything is going to be okay. You can too, no matter what traumatic experience you've encountered. The "I AM" Solution can change your victim experience into an empowering confirmation that your inner Hero exists regardless of the traumatic event. My story is The "I AM" Solution and how I transformed Fear back into Love.

Exercise Two

The act of writing in the "I AM" journal can be therapeutic and add to enlightenment. What were your thoughts while reading my story? When you were reading it, did it bring up any feelings and memories of when you felt helpless, trapped, victimized or even suicidal?

Reference

I've experienced challenges in my life where I blamed, accused and suffered to gain a higher perspective. I count it all as good now because I can see that the challenges were presented for me to unblock the light. Unforgiveness was blocking my light therefore I created more challenges that taught me to forgive. I've had loss of material things so I could discover that within me is the provider of all things. The "I AM" Solution is about turning trauma into triumph by the way we view the situation and our role in it.

In this video I talk about my journey and the mindset that needed to change in order to eliminate the victim mentality. Video, "Transforming Trauma to Triumph" at drkarmen.com

CHAPTER THREE

WHAT IS TRAUMA?

"Past trauma can create the current drama in our lives. The purpose for the drama is to either create limitations or break them."
~ Dr. Karmen

Trauma is a situation you experience as an immediate or chronic threat to yourself or others, sometimes followed by a wound which could be psychological and/or physical. The result of trauma includes feelings of terror or helplessness due to an inability to protect yourself from the outcome. These powerful, distressing emotions may be coupled with strong physical reactions, such as rapid heartbeat, trembling and stomach dropping. Psychologically, your world might stop making sense and you may feel as if you're in a dream state. Trauma can affect your emotional, developmental, psychological, behavioral, spiritual and physical functioning.

Due to the recent wars in the Middle East, Post Traumatic Stress Disorder (PTSD) has been a hot topic in the news. The Veterans Administration has been recruiting mental health providers due to the epidemic of PTSD diagnosed in the military. Soldiers are not the only people who experience trauma but they have brought it to the spotlight.

Many of us have experienced trauma through a divorce, bullying, the recession, losing a job, death of someone close, poor prognosis or natural disaster. All these life events can fit the description of trauma. They've shown up in my life and I know many of you may be in the midst of your cycle of suffering. What has been interesting to me is that some people experience traumatic events and use them to create abundance and joy, while others repeat the cycle of suffering throughout the generations.

So why is it that some experience trauma and yet live in abundance, love and joy while others are destroyed by trauma? The Cycle of Suffering is a fascinating phenomenon I've been studying for years within the Child Welfare System. I've researched what generates the Cycle of Suffering, how to overcome fear and the purpose of the learning process. One thing I know for sure is the importance of our self-identity. Knowing who we are is key to changing from the victim to the hero in your own story.

Trauma can be a repeating Cycle of Suffering that shows up in our life despite our best efforts to avoid it. While working in the Child Welfare System it appeared that all the pain and suffering of the world was showing up in the families I worked with. They had the same problems of larger societies but the problems had manifested to the point where these families could no longer safely care for their children. If there was prescription drug abuse in the larger society then it would show up in Child Welfare.

PTSD manifests as a series of **thoughts, feelings and actions** that could result in abuse and neglect within the family system. The result of the trauma experience can lead to domestic violence or directly to child abuse. Children come into protective custody when parents' traumas hinder their ability to keep their children safe.

When we seek power and control externally we tend to control those who are the most vulnerable. Thus we're creating the situations that cause physical and/or psychological safety risks to children and others who are vulnerable: the elderly, children, minorities and the environment become targets for the control seekers. Working within the Child Welfare setting created an excellent opportunity for me to study the causes and effects of trauma or suffering.

The children who come through Child Protective Services have one or multiple diagnoses such as Attention Deficit Hyperactivity Disorder (ADHD), Reactive Attachment Disorder (RAD), Oppositional Deviant Disorder (ODD), Explosive Outburst Disorder (EOD), encopresis, enuresis, autism, major depression, conduct disorder, PTSD, anxiety disorder and some are severely developmentally delayed. Many of these diagnoses can be traced to the events and environment they experienced at a young age or in utero. The trauma they suffered left them feeling helpless, fearful and powerless which perpetuated the behaviors/actions they exhibited.

The parents of these children have been diagnosed with major depression, PTSD, bipolar, anxiety disorder, developmentally delayed, attachment disorder, substance abuse and various personality disorders. These conditions can also be directly tied to their trauma experiences growing up or in utero. Trauma can also be passed down through the genes which lead to generational trauma. Recent research reveals that we can inherit trauma from our ancestors along with their positive coping strategies. It's vital to recognize that our fear can be transferred to our children. But, we can change our genes by transforming our Fear back to its original state of Love.

THE ALCHEMY OF TRAUMA.

Working with children who've experienced trauma has taught me that these events change the meaning we place on our identity. Yes, trauma has the ability to tell us who we are. We let it define us as victims which has a lasting effect. Based on what we **think/believe** affects what happens to us and directs the **actions/behavior** causing the **results/events** we experience as reality.

I believe children come into this world as curious, loving and gifted individuals still breathing the Spirit of the Divine. They're not a blank slate; I believe they possess a knowing that they're connected to something higher within them. They can't use words to describe this inner power but you can sense it if you observe infants and toddlers. They possess a love and knowing that's not tainted by the teaching of those who aren't awake to the power within all things. Children are here to be in joy with creation and to enjoy life.

Some people have had the experience of connecting with a baby without using words but with a feeling. You may use gibberish or baby talk but the baby reacts based on the feeling they're picking up from you and you react based on the feeling the baby is conveying. You're communicating based on feelings. Babies haven't forgotten that they're joy and love and this is how they interact with the world when their needs are met.

I've seen traumatic experiences change this innate connection and free spirit. When our hurt isn't valued or listened to it's replaced with fear, guilt, shame and anger. When we identify with the trauma or fear, our personality is defined by how to avoid it. The joyful identity is replaced with how to obtain and maintain power and control so we never experience our fears. When power and control are the main objectives we disconnect from our true self (love). This disconnect is displayed outwardly with power and control seeking **behaviors/actions.** An inner shift in identity is reflected in the **events/results** we created based on what we **believe/think** about ourselves and others. What we believe can show us how awesome and wonderful the world is (I AM) or how dangerous and fearful it is (Ego).

When working with children I've seen them create their world based on fear. When they experience trauma they can take on a victim mentality or personality. When they change their identity from victor to victim they act out in ways that result in more victimization.

> *"The kids who need the most love will ask for it in the most unloving ways."*
> ~Russel Barkley

I've also seen adults reconnect with their true Self and no longer see themselves as a victim. The formula for creating suffering is: what we **believe/think** creates a **feeling/emotion** which causes us to react and **action/behavior** brings **results/events** which create a chaotic cycle driven by fear. This blueprint is how we create our reality or illusion of suffering. We're creative beings and based on the vibration of our thoughts we create everything in our world.

Our **belief/thinking, feeling/emotion, behavior/action** and **events/results** process is illustrated in The Human Hamster Wheel. This cycle of suffering begins when we change our belief of who we are from victor to victim. The cycle can start generations before we're born, expand when we're young and by the time we're adults, it can be hardwired into our brain. When our brain is hardwired we've created a habitual form of thinking that's not easily broken. These habits become the beliefs that create patterns of suffering. We materialize people and objects that confirm our beliefs about ourselves and the world.

The good news is that you can employ conscious practices to renew authentic pathways and create inspired manifestations. We can change our brain back to its original state of wellbeing. *We can change the way we think, believe and feel!* The way we've been trained to end suffering is a delusion. We think by changing a situation or circumstance externally our suffering will be eliminated but that's not true. Whenever we change the result without changing the thought that caused it, we're delusional.

We can legislate equal rights for minorities, including the right to vote but it won't change the racist thoughts that created the system in the first place. When the thought is still intact, the end result will continue to have power and control over a minority group. Thoughts and intentions create results and these can't be legislated away. The thought has to be transformed first. When we hate others and don't see that it comes from a deep hatred of self, we see separation which doesn't exist. This is a delusional state of consciousness which is the Ego

We can also say that we're asleep, unconscious, sleepwalking or vibrating at a lower frequency. We become enlightened and awake when we consciously create experiences on a higher level of connected consciousness. We were created to have a life that ignites our highest self or inner Hero. By igniting our inner Hero we give others permission to create their life without fear writing every scene.

The Child Welfare System provided a perfect research environment to observe generational trauma or the cycle of suffering but this can also be generalized to the rest of the population. The cycle is relatable to anyone who's had difficult times and can see their own behavior in The Human Hamster Wheel. I participated in my own cycle of suffering for most of my life until I became aware I was creating it. It makes sense then if I AM causing, perpetuating and manifesting this cycle, I can also create based on the highest definition of Self. Only when I became awake to knowing my thoughts created my reality was I able to make conscious changes.

SECOND HAND TRAUMA

As a mental health therapist and an ordained minister I've had work experiences I can't talk about with family or friends. As a licensed professional I have confidentiality requirements that don't allow me to convey what someone discloses. The other reason I don't discuss what happens at work is that it could traumatize other people. Someone who hasn't chosen my line of work may be ill equipped to handle the second hand trauma that comes from hearing about suffering.

Being in the helping profession is a calling and for those who haven't been called it can be even more difficult to hear about the suffering we experience at work. The average person may watch the news and it changes their mood. But when you experience trauma as part of your job, you can suffer from chronic second hand trauma or compassion fatigue. This happens when you're exposed by listening to, reading about or witnessing trauma on a consistent basis. Those who've chosen to be a helping professional such as doctors, police officers, social workers and emergency responders tend to be isolated in their work related thoughts.

In 2007 I was in a car accident and suffered a concussion. I was off work for three months taking physical therapy and other treatments toward recovery. When I came back to work I went to my first staff meeting with a new supervisor. She was briefing the team of therapists and explained how she had responded to a crisis call and had to tell two children their mother was killed. She said the kids witnessed the shooting but weren't told what happened to her. The father was taken to jail for obstructing justice and the police officers responsible for the shooting brought the children to a shelter. My supervisor was very matter-of-fact and the other therapists listened without response. Inside I was devastated.

If I hadn't been on medical leave I would have had to disclose to the kids their mother's death. I was the one in my unit who answered crisis calls on a regular basis. But because I'd been off work for three months and had a head injury, I felt like I was stepping into someone else's life. That life appeared painful and traumatic. My first day back I worked half a day and was overwhelmed with emotions. I drove home in tears because as an empath, I felt the pain of the children. I'd lost all my built-up defenses which allowed me to do such an emotionally charged job. I had a direct experience of what it would be like if an average person walked into my job. It felt as if I'd never worked around trauma. My emotions were raw without a defense or filter.

Apparently my concussion had a serious impact on my ability to cope with second hand trauma. My job couldn't accommodate this disability, so I suffered through the daily traumas at work without the buffers I previously utilized. I experienced the children's pain of losing and seeing the murder of their mother without the boundary of professional distance. The concussion, my empathic abilities and leave of absence had wiped out all my defenses. I felt the trauma as if it was happening to me—helpless, powerless and traumatized through another's experience.

My head injury had a profound impact on me. Since my major in college was mental health research I never expected to be a lab rat in my own life. But that's exactly what happened after my injury—I wasn't the same person. I reacted to trauma much differently and that affected my personal and work life. I would listen to extreme trauma events and feel isolated holding onto the stories of the day. Work became a hostile place for me with back stabbing coworkers fueled by a vibrant gossip rumor mill. I would come home and complain about how stressful everything and everyone was and that *they* were doing it to me. This was out of character for me because before the accident I had a handle on it. Those around me could see I was stressed, tired and irritable. My fiancé and I were not in sync and my 17–year-old son had chosen to live with his father full time, cutting off all communication with me.

I had many physical ailments and despite several trips to the doctor the only diagnosis I received was that I was under stress. My mother and grandmother passed away in their early 50s from cancer so when I turned 50 I felt my days were numbered. When my physical symptoms were at their worst, my aunt, who's a doctor, demanded that I retire by the end of the year. I told her I would seriously look into the logistics of retiring. My work was stressful, my coworkers and fiancé weren't supportive and my son had disowned me. I struggled to find a cause to my physical pain but the doctors were clueless. Despite blood work, specialists and MRIs I never received a diagnosis let alone treatment. It was as if the Universe was trying to tell me something—yet I continued to look outside myself for the answer.

WAKE-UP CALL

The answer instinctively was not to quit my job which was what people were telling me to do. The answer was not to immediately and dramatically end my five-year relationship with my fiancé either. I knew the answer couldn't come from outside me. I was trying to get an external fix for an internal problem. First the answers had to come from me and not well-wishers or doctors. I realized my job had lost its meaning or more accurately I had lost my meaning. Since I AM the One who gives everything meaning, I felt I'd lost my true meaning or identity therefore everything around me didn't match my highest good. I felt useless and unimportant therefore my job was useless and unimportant. When I felt lifeless my job became an extension of those feelings.

My relationship amplified my sense of insecurity about the future and it made me feel unsafe and vulnerable. My son's disconnect was symbolic of how I had disconnected from my highest self. The Universe was showing me what needed to be realized. The changes needed to come from within me so I could manifest or reflect in the external realm my highest job, relationships and health. I lost sight of who I AM and why I AM here. I'd lost my way which is what trauma does. It causes us to lose our meaning and when that happens the meaning of everything in our life follows.

> *"It is by going down into the abyss that we recover the treasures of life.*
> *Where you stumble, there is your treasure."*
> ~ Joseph Campbell

Based on my years of studying metaphysics and psychological concepts I began to understand that I created the environment that was causing my body and emotions such stress. I know I AM the Creator of the situations I experience. I know I can create the space for abundance but not as long as I identify myself as a victim. In the past I would change my surroundings and people to improve my feelings of stress. This would always be a temporary fix because my identity didn't change. The same type of problems resurfaced only the characters and scenery would change.

☐ THOUGHTS/BELIEFS

I became aware that I was taking on the vibrational energy at work. This was helpless/victim energy which I was picking up mostly from my coworkers. I thought I wasn't being appreciated at work. I thought my fiancé wasn't taking care of me emotionally, financially and intellectually. I thought I was the victim of my work and family.

☐ FEELINGS/EMOTIONS

The helplessness created a feeling of powerlessness and from that came the fears: fear of being hurt, fear of not being loved or appreciated, feeling that I'm not enough, fear that something's wrong with me. My biggest fear was not feeling safe and secure.

☐ ACTION/BEHAVIOR

The physical reaction in my body was anxiety and stress. I had many pains and symptoms that couldn't be diagnosed. I tried to change my fiancé by telling him what I wanted him to change about himself. I wanted my son to do certain things but he saw it as nagging. I tried to have power and control over the behavior of others so they would stop stressing me. I blamed my work, fiancé, health and son for my anxiety.

☐ RESULT/EVENTS

My son cut off all communication with me. My fiancé began to resist and saw the relationship wasn't worth saving. My work became a place I dreaded going to every day. My grumpy angry demeanor at work conveyed I wasn't happy. My physical symptoms got worse and doctors' visits were futile.

As a result of this honest inventory I was able to recognize that I was creating the results I was getting. *I had to reach bottom before I looked within.* My bottom was when the Universe showed me I was repeating a pattern of suffering I experienced over and over in my life. I had to recognize: Hey there's a lesson here! I created and accepted the thoughts, feelings, actions and results I was creating. So changing the results like quitting my job wouldn't fix the problem. I had to start with my feelings and as an empath I AM particularly sensitive to the emotions of others. The emotions of powerlessness and victimization from another person affected me as if they were my own experiences of trauma.

I created The "I AM" Solution so I wouldn't have to take on the suffering of those around me. The "I AM" Solution is a way I can feel empathy and compassion for others without taking on and creating suffering from the trauma. This was a revelation that helped wake me up. There is a way of processing second hand or personal trauma that won't perpetuate The Human Hamster Wheel of Suffering

I didn't change my job and continued to work for the Child Welfare System; however now my job is fulfilling and a blessing. My fiancé is a friend after we decided not to get married. I was looking to him to fulfill a role that was meant for my inner Hero. My adult son returned when I released him from my expectations. He and I are spiritual partners symbolizing that I'd reconnected with my highest potential. To truly transform the root of trauma and stop the cycle of suffering we must go within and reclaim who we are.

The "I AM" Solution is a path to changing our fearful thoughts and victim identity back to love which leads to a life of abundance. The good news is that we're in an age of Enlightenment. Many spiritual and awakened people are spreading the word that our circumstances or events do not define us. They show us the path to creating everything we are. We're more than we know and we can be taught ways to identify with a definition of self that works for our highest potential.

Living a life of abundance and joy is The "I AM" Solution; it gets you off The Human Hamster Wheel of Suffering. On my journey I woke up to the fact that **I AM** everything I need. I had to ignite my inner Hero by transforming Fear back to Love.

Exercise Three

Look back at your life and list some milestones in your career, relationships and health. Are there challenges in any of these areas that are pointing you toward an inner solution? Have you made some inner changes and observed these external areas improve?

Reference

I've found throughout my work as a counselor those who have experienced trauma, forgiven and found their way to healing make the best counselors, hotline workers, first responders and caregivers. They have a personal connection and can empathize at a deeper level. These healers, because of their own trauma, respond in a way that joins the hurting person on the road to recovery and shows them the way out of suffering.

In this video I convey to a class at the University of Nevada, Las Vegas that once we learn the lesson we make the best teachers.
Video**,** "Nothing is Wasted" at drkarmen.com

CHAPTER FOUR

THE HUMAN HAMSTER WHEEL

"Opportunities to find deeper powers within ourselves come when life seems most challenging."
~ Joseph Campbell

As a Clinical Social Worker I assess the risks and strengths of families and determine interventions that would decrease the threat of harm to the child. The goal is to always help the family remain together while ensuring safety. When the risk factors are too high, the child is removed from the biological parents and placed in foster care or with a relative. After assessing hundreds of families over the years I discovered there are patterns of generational trauma. A pattern would emerge of abandonment, illegal activity, poverty, rape, homelessness, drug use, developmental delays, poor physical health, lack of education, constant moving and under-employment.

Patterns are results continued from one generation to the next. My colleagues experienced the same patterns of trauma when assessing families and were frustrated by the layers of generational suffering. Part of our job was to make recommendations that would address the pattern with services to allow reunification of the family. As part of the initial assessment process we obtained information about the family. What was most astonishing was that traumatic events were repeated in each generation. The grandparents experienced the same trauma the parents were experiencing in the present.

Repeating the cycle of suffering on a subconscious level is more common than one may think. When we mapped out the cycle of suffering on a white board in front of the families, the parents would be surprised to see a generational pattern emerge. They didn't want to repeat what their parents did but they could see they had. They never wanted to be an alcoholic like their father or have their children be raised by someone else, yet their children were removed because of their drug use. The same types of events the parents tried to avoid were showing up in the lives of their children.

Children Learn What They Live
by Dorothy Law Nolte, Ph.D.

If children live with criticism, they learn to condemn.
If children live with hostility, they learn to fight.
If children live with fear, they learn to be apprehensive.
If children live with pity, they learn to feel sorry for themselves.
If children live with ridicule, they learn to feel shy.

If children live with jealousy, they learn to feel envy.
If children live with shame, they learn to feel guilty.
If children live with encouragement, they learn confidence.
If children live with tolerance, they learn patience.
If children live with praise, they learn appreciation.
If children live with acceptance, they learn to love.
If children live with approval, they learn to like themselves.
If children live with recognition, they learn it is good to have a goal.
If children live with sharing, they learn generosity.
If children live with honesty, they learn truthfulness.
If children live with fairness, they learn justice.
If children live with kindness and consideration, they learn respect.
If children live with security, they learn to have faith in themselves and in those about them.
If children live with friendliness, they learn the world is a nice place in which to live.

THOUGHTS, FEELINGS, BEHAVIORS AND EVENTS.

The cycle of suffering is based on life events that can leave us feeling helpless and powerless. Those events dictate our thoughts, feelings and behavior. In the late 1990s I created The Human Hamster Wheel to better understand and teach this cycle of suffering to probation officers and Child Protective Services workers in the Department of Family Services. The diagram of the cycle of suffering makes every behavior coming from the ego understandable. The behaviors in society, at the time, appeared to be increasingly aggressive and self-destructive.

During that time school shootings, suicide bombers, gang violence and other senseless atrocities were happening with some frequency. I began to understand how trauma can create a sense of separation and isolation that can lead to acts of aggression. I created The Human Hamster Wheel as a framework to mark the beginning of my understanding of how insidious the events of trauma can be on the formation of our identity. What happens when we identify as being separate from others in society? The diagram addresses that question by showing that our behaviors can include self-destructive acts ranging from blaming and arguing to murder/suicide. All behaviors that derive from the cycle of suffering are a symptom of the larger problem, Fear, which leads to a loss of our true identity. This identity crisis causes us to lose our connection to humanity and to suffer the delusions that come from separation.

"Fear and the construct of the ego come from not knowing who we are."
~ Dr. Karmen

UNDERSTANDING THE CAUSE OF SUFFERING

All suffering comes from thinking we're separate, powerless and helpless. Trauma occurs when we experience a situation that triggers feelings of fear. When we remain in these feeling states, we're on The Human Hamster Wheel perpetuating our suffering. By using this model as a structure we can map out our pattern and make it easier to identify the thoughts, feelings, behaviors and results so we can transform them back to love. By transforming our identity we connect with the collective soul to change the world. Gandhi said, "Be the change you want to see in the world."

THE HUMAN HAMSTER WHEEL

As an intern, in order to accumulate clinical hours I conducted the adult groups at a psychiatric hospital. The clients had a range of diagnoses from schizophrenia to depression. Men and women from 18 to 70 were mandated to attend my group. I had to keep the clients entertained while offering insight. I had two goals: to make an impact and to not be heckled. I wanted to create a small crack in their consciousness for healing in the two hours I was allotted.

I anticipated the adult unit as being the toughest crowd a therapist-in-training could encounter. Some patients were taking medication that made them drowsy while others were anxious or actively delusional. So getting their attention or getting them to sit for five minutes was a challenge. I had observed other groups and the therapist would have a tough time keeping their attention and getting them to participate.

Talking in a group setting with chairs formed in a circle was never my style. So I decided to use a white board to help visualize the concepts I was conveying. I grew up in the television age so I'm a visual learner. If I can't see it I don't understand it. I used visual media to teach complicated paradigms. To this day I use video and other visuals in my lectures and online courses. I noticed that all the adults who came to my first group were interested in how the events in their lives led to feelings and behaviors and created the events that caused the fearful feelings. They were riveted by the simplicity of the patterns they'd created. By using The Human Hamster Wheel, they could see how all humans operate and that we create our own reality. The good news is that if we have the power to create these results we can change our reality by changing our thoughts. Change can happen now instead of waiting for the circumstance or situation to change. So at any time we can create a different reality. The adults in my group were able to pay attention and provide feedback which gave me encouragement to continue to develop the model.

EVENTS CAN CAUSE FEARFUL THOUGHTS

The first Human Hamster Wheel I created was tailored for the populations in Juvenile Detention, a mental health hospital unit and the child abuse and neglect shelter. These demographics provided a unique opportunity to view the pattern of suffering created by their **thoughts-feelings-behaviors-events.** Probation officers began requesting my model as a quick assessment tool that could provide them with a greater understanding of a child's behaviors and self-concept. After receiving a case, probation officers could circle the traumatic experiences, feelings, behaviors and results in a quick and concise manner. They could add events that weren't listed on the chart along with feelings and behaviors specific to their clients.

While working in the clinical unit responding to calls from the boys unit in Juvenile Detention, I took note of trauma patterns. I was usually responding to the boys units where the kids showed signs of depression, anxiety and sometimes psychosis. There were recurring themes that continued to appear when the teen boys were telling their story. The stories consistently contained these major trauma triggers:

ABANDONMENT: Loss of one or both parents can be a significant life-changing event. The loss of the male role model can lead to aggression in males. The teen was oftentimes being raised by extended family or on the streets with gangs as their fictive kin or substitute for biological relatives.

SICK CAREGIVER: There seemed to be a sick parent with chronic or terminal illness. The sick caregiver could have been an addict, depressed, obese or with a disability. The child experienced a parent that wasn't fully able to provide emotional support due to physical or mental limitations.

CONSTANTLY MOVING: Some of the teens appeared to have moved from location to location due to evictions, military parents, changing primary caregivers or repeated incarcerations.

PHYSICAL AND SEXUAL ABUSE: Physical abuse was caused by family or from gang related assaults or bullying behavior at school.

EMOTIONAL ABUSE: Emotional abuse included but was not limited to name calling, racial profiling, social media attacks, witnessing domestic violence and being disrespected in any relationship. Critical self-talk that enforces fear-based thinking can be emotionally abusive.

DISABILITY: Learning disabilities and physical and mental processing challenges can be identity changing. There's a big dropout rate within juvenile detention which may be due to undiagnosed learning disabilities.

These events shaped how the boys saw themselves and the world around them. It appeared that these traumatic events contributed to their criminal acts, gang involvement, aggression, negative environment, theft and drug selling. The teens seemed to be self-destructive and have a disconnect from humanity. They tended to make villains out of other people for little or no reason. They were angry with everyone including themselves. The years of chronic and generational suffering created events that verified their fears of loss, separation and revenge. These thoughts were all self-destructive leading to events that furthered the cycle of suffering.

THE PATTERN THAT ABANDONMENT CAN CAUSE

Many people have experienced some form of abandonment. It could be in the form of an emotionally absent parent—one who's physically around but is emotionally detached. The adult doesn't encourage the child because he/she is withdrawn or working all the time. The physical absence of the father in boy's life can be significant and there have been many studies to suggest that males can become more aggressive and angry as well as believe they're not good enough.

Some of the teens in detention had children themselves they'd abandoned. One teen was 17 and had two children by two different girls and even though he vowed he would never leave his kids like his father did, he wasn't involved in his kids' lives. How could that happen? How can we repeat something knowing how it made us feel? The teens explained how they wouldn't repeat what was done to them but they were repeating the exact cycle of suffering. None of them were aware of the obvious fact that they were doing the same thing that was done to them. All used blame and denial to cloud the truth.

Some would blame the judicial system, the mother of their children—even an unfair eviction. By blaming and denying their abandonment they didn't have to face their fear. By not facing their fear of abandonment they were re-creating it with their children. They were repeating the generational cycle of suffering. The ability to be unconscious to our part in creating our life is a fairly common occurrence.

Let's take a closer look at this recurring cause observed in Juvenile Detention: Abandonment. **Abandonment** is a traumatic event in the life of children. They **believe** the reason the person left is because there's something wrong with them; they're flawed, unlovable, unworthy and unimportant. Children aren't born with these beliefs; they're taught them through external experiences. After the experience there's an inner identity shift that takes on a feeling of helplessness and powerlessness which creates fear. The **behaviors** of self-destruction are evidence of the inner identity belief system. The Human Hamster Wheel can trace the outer experiences and behavior back to the inner identification and false belief which need to be transformed. If the inner thoughts aren't transformed, the results will continue to show up as trauma, drama and as the Kabbalists say chaos.

"By impersonating the aggressor, assuming his attributes or imitating his aggression, the child transforms himself from the person threatened to the person who makes the threat."
~ Anna Freud, 1941

Anna Freud discovered the transformative power of trauma. Trauma can transform us into victims who then try to assume external power by becoming one who victimizes others. Early trauma can create a lifetime of seeking external power and control that not only hurts others but is detrimental to ourselves. We begin to habitually seek outside power by using the behaviors on The Human Hamster Wheel. In our culture we're taught that seeking external power by accumulating things makes us superior to others. So if your core fear **belief** is "not being good enough" or "not being accepted", the behavior may be to seek external power and control by using one of the behaviors on the Wheel to gain superiority. The outside world appears to support this way of seeking power and control.

If you look at the housing bubble and Wall Street investors' involvement linked with the desire to accumulate the bigger, more expensive home you'll see a recipe for disaster. Investors, bankers and homeowners, you could argue, were trying to seek external power and control by manipulation. This way of seeking power and control isn't part of our true nature but comes from a feeling of lack which creates an intention to get more by any means necessary. Sometimes in a capitalist society, happiness is defined by "the person with the most toys wins". In terms of the housing bubble, in particular, one could say that greed and a fear of lack drove the market. The recession, or correction, was caused by all involved gaining gratification using deceitful practices to accumulate wealth. These thoughts and fear-based **beliefs** are contrary to the original essence of our identity which contains an inner power that's herculean and not dependent on the material for self-worth. The alchemy which changes us from inner Hero to insecure people chasing imitations of power and control is **suffering**.

GENERATIONAL PATTERNS OF SUFFERING

Patterns are generated by our fearful thoughts that make up our ego. We create fear beliefs that reflect our view of the world and who we are in it. Fearful beliefs define our false self. False beliefs are instigators and provide the energy to perpetuate The Human Hamster Wheel. Fear can be passed from generation to generation. When a parent has a fear belief that they're not good enough and identifies with low self-worth due to early abandonment experiences, they may leave their child as their parent may have left them. And that child may grow up and be a parent who leaves their children.

The abandonment experience creates the same types of fears which perpetuate the cycle of suffering through the generations. Both the parent's and child's identity become that of a victim. The child grows up hating the parent while the parent has guilt toward the child which creates the result of continued suffering. Both view themselves as the victim reminded of their feelings by the other's existence.

When we identify ourselves as victims (victim identity formation) we create fear-based emotional reactions to most of life's experiences. What most people don't realize is that they're creating with this fear-based belief system the very victim results they say they don't want. Fear-based behaviors will be repeated until the underlying identity belief changes. The ability to see these patterns and how they've affected our lives can be a cathartic experience for people ready to change. The Human Hamster Wheel provides a simple visual tool that can help with this process.

THE HUMAN HAMSTER WHEEL OF SUFFERING

Power and Control

Reactions
Blaming
Shaming
Lying
Manipulating
Arguing
Being addicted
Judging
Criticizing
Controlling
Mentally detach
Isolating
stress related illness
Physically assaulting self and others
Homicidal / Suicidal

Fear

Events
Death
Bullied
Divorce
Emotional
Physical abuse
Rape
Financial crisis
Disability
Abandonment
Natural Disaster
War
Domestic violence
Physical pain
Betrayed
Culture
Frequent moves

Feelings
Hurt/Afraid
Powerless
Angry
Guilty/ Ashamed

IT'S SOMEBODY ELSE'S FAULT

Two of the major behavioral reactions to fear are **blame** and **denial**. Blame is one of the reactions used to deflect the attention away from inner vision. It's the major reaction that stunts our spiritual growth. When we deflect our attention by blaming others we fail to take the inner journey that leads to transformation. Blame keeps us looking for an outside solution to an inside problem.

When we blame others we're not using our authentic power, abdicating it to someone else. So we're once again powerless to change our situation. Instead we rely on other actions on The Human Hamster Wheel such as lying, manipulating and criticizing. These reactions to the triggers don't give power, only the illusion of power and control. As long as we remain disconnected from our true self this delusion of power is all we know.

The Human Hamster Wheel generates just enough energy to last for a short time. We feel as if we're in control but it's fleeting. It's not sustainable, so another act has to happen in order to keep feeling powerful. This cycle can form the personality traits of the individual stuck going nowhere like a hamster on a wheel. **Events** happen; then **feelings** are triggered and based on our fears; **behaviors** follow which create similar **results**. When thoughts are fearful we're stuck on the Hamster Wheel, which limits our behavior and results. We're going through life in fear instead of in joy; we're creating this fearful way of living with the EGO.

THE HUMAN HAMSTER WHEEL OF SUFFERING

EVENTS
Death
Abandonment
Physical Abuse
Emotional Abuse
Sexual Abuse
Environment Negative
Domestic Violence
Addiction
Sick Caregiver
Constantly Moving
Poverty
Over Abundance
Music/ Movies/ Video Games/ Internet
Disability
Natural Disaster
Financial loss
War

FEELINGS
Anger
Depression
Guilt
Shame
Rage
Insecure/Helpless
Powerless

POWER AND CONTROL REACTIONS
Blaming
Lying
Criticizing
Arguing
Mentally Detaching
Judging
Manipulating
Destroying Property
Stealing
Addiction
Runaway/Constantly Moving
Physical and Mental Illness
Incarceration
Quitting
Isolating
Self-Inflicted Abuse
Assault/ Rape
Homicide
Suicide

Exercise Four

Complete your own Human Hamster Wheel. Fill in the events, feelings and power and control reactions on the blank Human Hamster Wheel provided.

Reference

The Human Hamster Wheel was developed to address the question: How do we block the light of God? I'd known that

EGO can be considered an acronym for Edging God Out but I wanted to know more about the ego. I discovered it wants to have power and control in ways unlike God. The ego uses manipulation, anger, blame and all sorts of tools to gain power and control over a situation or person. The Human Hamster Wheel is a pattern that recycles the same hurt and pain creating more of the same until we awaken to love.

In this video I show the pattern of suffering the ego creates which is The Human Hamster Wheel.
Video, "The Human Hamster Wheel" at drkarmen.com

THE HUMAN HAMSTER WHEEL OF SUFFERING

List the hurtful events in your life
The feelings that followed
and your Power and Control Reactions.

Power and Control Reactions **Events**

Feelings

CHAPTER FIVE

F.E.A.R. = FROM EGO ALTERING REALITY

"The only thing to FEAR is fear itself."
~ Franklin D. Roosevelt

Looking behind the curtain and exposing the wizard is beneficial in understanding that our fears, oftentimes, are not real. One of my favorite movies growing up was *the Wizard of Oz*. I came to know later the spiritual significance and the universal messages of fear and love that are symbolized in the movie.

The story begins with Toto being taken away by the mean woman, who didn't like Dorothy or her little dog. In order to hurt Dorothy she tried to shame her by saying mean things so she wouldn't see herself as good. The traumatic event came when Toto was taken and Dorothy was heartbroken. Toto, fearless dog that we was, jumped out of the woman's bicycle bag and ran back to Dorothy. Toto represented Dorothy's highest self—a loving, fearless, smart presence. Of course along her spiritual path, she encountered three attributes symbolized in the scarecrow who felt he wasn't smart, the tin man who felt he had no heart (or feeling) and the cowardly lion who was afraid of his own shadow and desired courage.

One of the scariest scenes in the movie for me was when they went to see the GREAT AND POWERFUL Wizard of Oz. Everyone was scared—the scarecrow, the tin man, Dorothy and most of all the cowardly lion—except Toto. Toto, the true identity of Dorothy, went to the curtain and pulled it back to reveal an old man pulling levers and pushing buttons. The dog showed there was nothing to be afraid of and the attributes of intelligence, love and courage were there all along—behind the fear. The Wizard and the witch turned out to be nothing but illusions manifested from the false belief of lack. Along Dorothy's journey, Toto (representing her inner Hero) was prompting her to the realization that Fear is just From Ego Altering Reality (F.E.A.R.). The people of OZ didn't need a Wizard but because they were afraid, they forgot their inner power. When we forget our own power we put ourselves in a position to be controlled and victimized. The good news is that there's a hero in our story and it's us. Thanks Toto.

WHAT LIES BEHIND THE CURTAIN?

The surface personality is being controlled by fearful thoughts. Our soul (inner Hero) wants to show the personality that without our fear we're limitless beings filled with unlimited potential. Fear is limiting and destructive and leads to a finite expression. The expression of the ego is limited to the spokes on The Human Hamster Wheel. Our manifestations based on fear are limited to drama, chaos, trauma and self-destruction which perpetuate the circular momentum.

When we feel fear, our identity is at its most vulnerable. This is why all religions of the world teach: We should fear not. Fear sets in motion lies that we believe to be true contributing to the delusion. When we believe the lie that we're broken and that there's something wrong with us we become dependent and addicted to the result of the ensuing chaos which gives the illusion of fixing it. Drama queen is a popular term for people addicted to the drama they create. This pattern hinders us from recognizing our wholeness and drowns out our inner Hero who speaks in silence.

"The whole secret to existence is to have no fear. Never fear what will become of you, depend on no one. Only the moment you reject all help are you freed."
~ Buddha

Let's look at how fear can creep in like a virus and take over our belief system. Follow along on the diagram of The Human Hamster Wheel to chart the cycle of suffering.

<u>INITIAL WOUNDING (EVENT)</u>: The Human Hamster Wheel of Suffering.

A little girl named Skyler wants the attention of her father but he's too busy to play. He's working long hours and is stressed when he eventually comes home. He's driven by his fear of not being enough and becoming the failure his father thought he would be. He's not aware of anything that doesn't reflect back his lack of outer success. Therefore he can't see his daughter's love.

FORMATION OF THE FEARFUL BELIEF

Skyler internalizes the lack of play and attention as "he doesn't love me". When she seeks her father's attention through interrupting him, he becomes agitated and shames her for her actions. She hears her parents argue over money and she internalizes the feeling of lack. Her father stays away from the house more and more and when he's around the doors slam. When her father is home her parents argue. He then leaves the family through divorce. Skyler believes there's something wrong with her. She didn't feel love from her father and his total absence is confirmation that it's true: "He never loved me."

FEAR of loss, abandonment, not being good enough, not lovable, not being pretty.

As Skyler grows up her sadness turns to depression. She believes she's not beautiful when she sees magazine covers and other media. Her feelings of not being good enough are familiar and become a part of her vocabulary. She feels depressed most of the time but covers it over in social situations.

BEHAVIORS/ACTIONS.

She chalks her failed relationships up to the fact that men don't want serious or long-term commitments. Her job is something she hates. Workplace difficulties and other drama-filled events show up in her life.

EVENTS/RESULTS.

Her beliefs about her identity were initiated in childhood and confirmed by the life events she manifested in adulthood. Looking at her life she had failed relationships and endured emotionally abusive men. Her self-talk was about beating herself up and her mother would ask why she let men treat her so badly. So she stopped telling her mom about her relationships. She believes she needs to change her job, her appearance or meet the right guy in order to gain what she's missing. She tries to change all those external veneers. She continues to have unsatisfying relationships and still doesn't like the way she looks. Once again she listens to the world for answers. She finds herself buying something to make her happy. Meanwhile the inner belief of unworthiness, of not being lovable and of not being enough is embedded in her identified personality. A culture driven by consumption profits from her "dis-ease" about herself. The marketing machines capitalize on her demographic. She buys more and more things because she's chasing an external fix for an internal fear of loss. She thinks if she buys enough stuff or the right thing it will help her get the results she wants. It becomes a bottomless pit which can't seem to be filled.

> *"If you don't define yourself then there will always be something or someone to do it for you."*
> ~ Dr. Karmen

Traumatic experiences can generate the fear of being unworthy, unlovable, not good enough, not valued and being broken. These fears are lies yet we could spend our lives generating more experiences that would confirm our beliefs. The Universe however gives us opportunities along the way to change our beliefs every time a trauma event is manifested. There's only One consciousness which is not made up of fear. When we're operating from the ego we're manifesting suffering. And yes, we can change our beliefs based on our Divine awakening. Each human being may have different experiences but the intentions are the same. All experiences on The Human Hamster Wheel are calls to ignite your inner Hero by exposing the lies. We're not lacking anything, so the fearful thoughts aren't true until we feel them and act on them. When we turn inward we return to the Love, Gratitude and Compassion which are in our heroic toolbox of emotions.

We're constantly getting messages from our childhood, the media, culture and relationships about who we are—and we believe them. We believe these outer messages consciously or unconsciously. If we thought we were dumb in school and we felt inferior, it will show up as events created by the feared belief. If we believe we're not worthy or we're unlovable then we materialize relationships and events that confirm this belief.

WE FORM OUR IDENTITY THROUGH NEWS, MOVIES AND CULTURE.

I remember seeing on the news a church that was bombed. The camera showed the rubble and pictures of little Black girls who were inside the church at the time of the explosion. They were attending Sunday school and a bomb was planted by the white fear-based group: the KKK. I was six and afraid to go to church. During the 1960s, news coverage showed dogs attacking and water hoses being used to hurt Black men, women and even kids. I was traumatized. I felt helpless, powerless and thought my life was in danger. I thought if "officer friendly" (we were taught in school police officers were officer friendly) is doing this to Black people, then I must be bad.

The television was my babysitter then and I was hooked. I would watch the Vietnam War and the civil rights movement from my living room. I watched movies with negative stereotypes where the Black character's eyes would get big to show he was scared, while the white character would save the day. There were no Black heroes, She-roes, Kings or Princesses. If there was a small Black role the character would get killed off early, do something morally wrong or be labeled a criminal. The older black and white movies depicted white people living in opulent mansions while the Blacks were uneducated servants.

My mother had an idea that these images were affecting the way I viewed myself and she was right. She introduced me to Black poets and inventors to replace the negative images I'd been exposed to but the damage was done. The larger American culture saw me as inferior based on the color of my skin and I internalized these fears at a young age.

You may be familiar with the famous "Black doll" study that was conducted in the 1940s which had a major implication in the "Brown vs. the Board of Education" Supreme Court decision. The study looked at doll preference in the segregated South with Black children and found a white bias. The preference toward white was related to the separate schools and unequal treatment of Blacks and whites during that time. You might not be surprised to know that a new study found that both Black and white kids were biased toward lighter skin dolls.

"The test in 2010 was aimed to recreate the landmark doll study of the 1940s. A white child looks at a picture of a Black child and says she's bad because she's black. A white child says a Black child is dumb because she has darker skin. Nearly 60 years after American schools were desegregated and more than a year after electing the country's first Black president, white children have an overwhelming white bias and Black children have a bias toward whites," according to the study commissioned by CNN. Renowned child psychologist and University of Chicago professor Margaret Beale Spencer, a leading researcher in the field of child development concluded, "We are still living in a society where dark things are devalued and white things are valued."

Police shootings of Blacks sparked the "Black Lives Matter" campaign in 2014. This campaign wanted to address the bias that police officers have against Black people. Riots that target minority neighborhoods instead of white areas of town can be related to this preference toward whites. Black on Black crime may be an example of self-hatred.

FEAR OF BEING STUPID

When I was in fifth grade, on the first day of school the teacher gave the students a test. The seating chart was made based on how we scored. The kids with the lowest scores were on one side of the room and those with the higher scores were on the other side. There was an isle in the middle that separated the students based on their scores. The schools in Kansas City were newly desegregated and Blacks were being bussed to the white area of town to attend the elementary school. My teacher had found a way to segregate her classroom. She had Blacks on one side and whites on the other. The teacher turned her back to the Black students and lectured to the white students.

In the beginning of the school year I raised my hand to give an answer and the teacher told me that the answers could only come from the other side of the room. She turned her back to me and called on a white student for the answer. About two weeks into the school year my side of the room was used to being ignored. I learned not to ask questions so I stopped raising my hand. She wasn't teaching us, listening to us or acknowledging those on my side so we mentally checked out. I daydreamed and doodled at my desk while others talked and passed notes. They would get in trouble and be sent to the office for disrupting the other side of the room.

The "I AM" Solution

Bussing was a hot topic in Kansas City and in most cities around the country. Our family moved to a white neighborhood in the 1970s and I walked to school. Some white people would drive by yelling "nigger" out their window. The store employees would follow me around as if my skin color meant I was a thief. I was too young to know just how racist the school seating chart was. I didn't know how detrimental the negative name calling and television images would be on the formation of my identity. They all influenced my thoughts about the world and my role in it. I learned in my fifth grade class that I was stupid, not to ask questions and to look to someone else for the answers. I was visually taught every day at school that Black people aren't smart, some white people hate me because of my skin color and authority figures devalue me.

I definitely developed an inferiority complex as a result of my school experiences, watching television and growing up in an all-white neighborhood. My fear of not being good enough grew as I attended junior high and high school with the same group of kids. The classroom was never a good experience for me because I believed I was stupid, unimportant and not worth listening to. I began to create events based on these beliefs of low self-worth and inferior intellectual capabilities.

FEAR CAN CREATE JUST LIKE LOVE CAN

I created, outside of my awareness, situations that would trigger those feelings that identified me as unimportant, stupid and invisible. School terrified me, so going to college was going to be a break down or a break through experience. The fear of being humiliated like I was in fifth grade made my heart beat out of my chest. I remember enrolling in one class at community college: abnormal psychology. I sat in the front row so nothing would block my teacher's face; I had his full attention. He was engaging, the topic was riveting and I began slowly replacing some of my fearful thoughts and feelings. I had to confront my fear and answer the call to study psychology instead of avoiding my demons.

Deep insecurities can create a doorway for future victimization. We can lose the ability to trust our thoughts, feelings and actions. We may become immobilized with fear, devaluing the gifts and talents we were given. We then wait for others to give us value and meaning which is a set up for more victim results.

PATTERNS OF FEAR

You may be familiar with the story of Job in the Bible that depicts a faithful believer of God who is given, what I like to call, the love test. His life is filled with one traumatic event after the other, including the death of his family and loss of his livelihood. Job reaches the dark night of the soul where he questions why he was born. When he experiences these thoughts of despair, he reflects and comes to the following realization: *"For the thing which I greatly fear comes upon me and that of which I am afraid befalls me."* Job 3:25

He had the realization that his fears were having a direct effect on his experiences. Only when he saw the truth—that his fears were orchestrating his experiences—was he able to replace them with faithful thoughts along with the corresponding feeling. When he uttered the passage above he had come to the cathartic awareness that he had to consciously change his thinking in order to change his reality. Once he connected with the God Consciousness or inner Hero he was showered with abundance. Stepping into the I AM presence reveals that fear was the instigator the entire time and this is a key to the awakened life.

We can all be like Job and have the divine revelation that can change generations of suffering into joy and abundance. We can reclaim our true definition of ourselves by knowing fear is not a part of our birthright. Fear dictates what we experience on a daily and generational basis only when we're not aware of it.

REPEATING THE "TRAUMA DRAMA"

When we become familiar with suffering through generational exposure or our own created pattern, it can feel like our life is not in our control. After chronic suffering of one kind or another chaos seems normal. One of the biggest red flags to a therapist is when people tell the most horrendous, violent, traumatizing story and say it as though it was the most "normal" thing. These patients may even justify it by saying it happens to everybody. The drama and trauma became an expected part of life for them. They may have had to go to detention or had the police called to their house several times and therefore convinced themselves that this happens to everyone. They were unable to safely navigate these events which they thought randomly happened in their lives. The truth is the minefield was not the events but their mind, thoughts and intentions that made up the field.

Some people get great pleasure—and an ego boost—from telling their story of suffering, gaining sympathy from the listener. Telling their story of suffering confirms the victim paradigm which perpetuates the cycle of suffering. Iyanla Vansant, a spiritual teacher and author, explains that when someone is telling their victim story it's as if they're taking a shot of drugs in order to get high.

The high she refers to comes from the sympathy people show which offers temporary connection. This compassion gives them a shot of feeling loved, that someone cares. The trauma and drama they create from their fearful thoughts of lack and being unloved will multiply in order to get the same sympathy fix. They've created an external way of gaining self-worth by telling their victim story.

These stories of suffering become their identity and calling card. Until they stop telling and believing their story nothing will change. They're so connected to it that they're resistant to change. By telling the victim story they connect with suffering and no one can fix the problem. The person's thoughts confirm their challenge can never be remedied. They may say they want help and may even read self-help books but they're addicted to suffering to gain sympathy and love, to feel that external connection.

They create a superficial bond with people through their suffering. Instead of being a giver they're constantly receiving which drains family and service providers. When nothing changes, they have more victim experiences to share which perpetuates the cycle of suffering (HHW). Even when someone helps them improve the result of their suffering they may not see things as getting better because it doesn't fit their habitual thought pattern. This person may say they want help but their thoughts have convinced them this is their fate.

LET'S THROW MONEY AT IT

Our society looks at the created result and attempts to fix it with the same belief system that created it. This way of problem solving doesn't create lasting change; it's like stuffing a leak with toilet paper. The toilet paper will stop the water for a short time until it's saturated and begins to leak again. Sometimes in the helping profession the therapist can exert much effort but sometimes nothing really changes within the family. Just when you think one thing is fixed something else breaks apart and needs your attention.

I began working in the helping profession in the late 1980s as a family support worker. I worked with families to improve their parenting skills and support them in their efforts toward becoming more stable. What I discovered right away was their needs were great and even when the needs were filled, another would appear. Providing services sometimes seemed like trying to fill a bottomless pit.

I remember during my work when several homeless people were given a beautiful apartment. They needed a nice place to live, food and clothing which were all provided without cost. However, no other services were provided. The home was trashed shortly after moving in. In other instances, within a short time a women who finally left an abusive relationship found themselves back in another one or the same abusive relationship months later. When we throw money at a problem without changing the thoughts that created the result, we haven't solved the pattern of suffering. The beliefs and pattern of thoughts that are held unconsciously cause the cycle of trauma. When the thoughts remained intact— even though the home was provided for the homeless and the abusive relationships ended—the results will always confirm the beliefs. The same type of victim thinking remains and creates future suffering.

As a social worker I believe tangible resources are important but I don't believe outer fixes will change a deep seated belief in victimization. The belief that we're victims steals our power and ability to change our result. When a person believes they're helpless to change, then that belief becomes their reality. In order to transform from victim to victor there has to be a conscious identity change. We can only change the outward manifestation of problems through our inner belief that materialized it. In other words we have to understand that what we experience is giving us opportunities to focus on our inner thoughts and beliefs.

As long as we focus on the outer problem it reinforces the victim identification. Instead, the therapeutic question should be: WHO ARE YOU? Focusing objectively on our fear, which is where the feelings and behaviors come from, is the key to establishing true change. The solution needs to be in reclaiming the identity we were born with.

The "I AM" Solution is about returning to the highest identity of self. Once we connect with our inner Hero, our thoughts and behaviors begin to reflect this powerful identity. The "I AM" Solution has helped me move beyond the cycle of suffering I created. When The "I AM" Solution is realized problems evaporate because the Universe has raised a mirror to show us our fear-based beliefs (The Human Hamster Wheel). Once we reclaim our identity, the clarity is so beautiful that we fall in love with who we are and feel connected to everything around us. We can then manifest from that space of power rather than victimhood.

WHEN THERE IS NO AWARENESS THERE IS NO CHANGE.

The definition of insanity is to continue thinking the same way and doing the same thing and expecting a different outcome. The best example I've ever heard to describe this is when we're on an elevator wanting to go to the 6th floor. We push the 2nd floor button, the door opens on the 2nd floor and we're disappointed that it's not the floor we want. We try again wondering how the mistake was made: we want 6 but push 2 and the doors close briefly and reopen on the same floor. Can you imagine how frustrated and angry you would feel if this continued to happen over and over again. We would blame the elevator, the building and the buttons—anything other than our part in the cycle. This is the definition of insanity. You want a specific outcome but you keep thinking, feeling and doing the same thing expecting the results to be different.

In order to change the results it's imperative that we identify the fears we believe are true. When our fear is triggered, it will trigger a feeling: anger, guilt, sadness etc. When we feel these emotions, it's a signal that we have a fear that needs to be brought to our awareness. The fears that drive our emotions and behavior have to be revealed to be healed.

I've listed some fears below and have underlined the one that challenged me. Be brave like Toto and underline the fears that keep you on The Human Hamster Wheel of Suffering. Increase your awareness by bringing FEAR to the surface.

FEARS:

Fear of being unlovable
<u>Fear of being worthless</u>
<u>Fear of being broken or needing to be fixed</u>
Fear of not being deserving of love
Fear of not being pretty or handsome enough
Fear of being alone
<u>Fear of not being accepted</u>
<u>Fear of being rejected</u>
<u>Fear of not being enough</u>
Fear of being yourself
<u>Fear of being judged</u>
<u>Fear of success</u>
<u>Fear of failure</u>
Fear of not being liked

Fear of being crazy
Fear of intimacy
Fear of death
Fear of making a mistake
Fear of taking risks
Fear of trusting
Fear of being shamed
Fear of confrontation
Fear of life
Fear of the unknown
Fear of being criticized or blamed
Fear of being betrayed
Fear of being condemned
Fear of being stupid
Fear of abandonment
Fear of being hurt
Fear of being exposed
Fear of not being safe
Fear of being who you REALLY are

WHY ARE MY FEARS SO HARD TO GET RID OF?

The latest brain research shows that the primal or early brain structures (like the amygdala) are in charge of the fight or flight response. The amygdala plays a key role in the processing of emotions. We're wired to have a fear response for a short period of time to insure survival. In the animal kingdom, for example, when a lion is hungry and approaches a zebra, the nervous system in the zebra's fight or flight reaction is activated and the animal will respond to the threat by running away. When the lion has given up the chase and the zebra determines he's no longer in danger, the amygdala is no longer activated and will relax. Humans, on the other hand, will hold onto the fear and form memories and beliefs associated with that trauma. We form emotions surrounding the initial fear such as anger, resentment, frustration and anxiety. We continue to associate these emotions with the initial fearful thought. Our brain stores this emotional baggage because it's protecting us from possible re-injury. Then we create more traumatic events triggering the initial fear. We don't want to face our fear because it can be painful to bring to the light of day. Long held fears of not being good enough or lovable, or of being stupid, lie in wait for the next trigger. It can be our boss, fiancé, spouse or child who says something that triggers the emotional reaction and behavior.

When the initial trauma event happens, feelings of helplessness are stored along with the initial fear. These emotions, when triggered later by similar events, will keep us stuck in a perpetual state of helplessness. We then try to avoid the events we create by using reactions like blame and aggression. Most of us are unaware of this law of avoidance which Job talked about in the Bible. The more we use these power and control reactions to avoid our fear, the more we create the trauma events.

FEAR EMOTIONS AND YOUR BODY

Holding onto the emotions attached to fear can produce stress hormones like cortisol and adrenaline which can cause physical and mental health problems. High blood pressure, cancer, addictions, depression, anxiety and autoimmune disorders are among those health issues that can be caused by the emotions triggered by fear. Holding onto these emotions are specifically a human characteristic. As we spin on The Human Hamster Wheel which is generated by our fearful thoughts, we self-inject suffering into our body. Our suffering doesn't just affect us but the global community. This ripple effect creates the result of world suffering in the form of global warming, slavery, genocide and world chaos.

The "I AM" Solution reminds us to turn within to Love and Compassion instead of fear. The alchemy of turning Fear back to Love will create a connection to all living beings and the environment. The ultimate healing choice is to give a loving response rather than reacting on an intention to avoid what makes us most afraid.

FEAR IS A PREDICTABLE PATH

I mentioned earlier that my son appeared on this planet as a big expression of love. This was obvious to me and I wanted to cultivate this love and not destroy it. If I parented him the way I was raised, he would have to navigate through pathways of fear. So when I was aware and not stressed by work, money and day care, I tried to parent differently. I looked for visual and cultural ways to describe spiritual concepts. I wanted him to know that within him is everything he needs and that he could access it through his understanding of himself. When he was about two years old he fell in love with the *LION KING* movie. He would watch it repeatedly. The *Lion King* is based on an African story which teaches that we come from royalty therefore within us is a King or Queen. No matter what life brings remember Who You Are. The Lion King reminds us of the truth that our life is not determined by circumstances but by who we know we are. At any given moment we can believe we are brave, wise or loving. Or we can believe the slanderous thoughts that come from fear, guilt and shame.

My son and I love movies, so showing him the visual along with the metaphorical meaning was important to me. George Lucas used many ideas from Joseph Campbell's *The Hero's Journey* in the making of the *Star Wars* movies. Joseph Campbell described the hero's journey as a basic pattern found in many narratives around the world. This pattern was described in Campbell's book *The Hero with a Thousand Faces* (1949). Campbell discovered that numerous myths from around the world share the same fundamental structure and stages: "A hero ventures forth from the world of common day into a region of supernatural wonder; fabulous forces are encountered and a decisive victory won; the hero comes back from this mysterious adventure with the power to bestow boons on his fellow man."

Campbell further contended that if the hero returns successfully, the boon or gift may be used to improve the world. The stories of Osiris, Prometheus, Moses, Gautama Buddha, Simba (*Lion King*), Luke Skywalker (*Star Wars*), Neo (*Matrix*) and Jesus for example, follow this structure closely.

The concept of higher consciousness is shown in the *Star Wars* movies. Once, when I lectured at University of Nevada Las Vegas on The Human Hamster Wheel, my son helped teach the fear segment of my seminar. He was about five and he memorized Yoda's famous words when speaking to the young apprentice. The lines are from *STAR WARS: EPISODE I - THE PHANTOM MENACE*. The young apprentice is being interviewed by the Jedi counsel, a person trained to be One with the Force.

Yoda: How feel you?
Apprentice: Cold sir.
Counsel member: You are worried about your mother.
Apprentice: I miss her.
Yoda: Afraid to lose her I bet.
Apprentice: What's that got to do with anything?

(My son at five would say Yoda's lines below and then explain the meaning.)

Yoda: Everything. *Fear is the path to the dark side. Fear leads to anger, Anger leads to hate and hate leads to suffering.* I sense much fear in you.

Those who are familiar with the *Star Wars* movies know that the young apprentice grows up to become Darth Vader, the dark lord. In *Star Wars: Episode I - the Phantom Menace*, Yoda could sense the fear and anger in the young apprentice and could predict his path. Yoda knew the transformative power of the thoughts and emotions the young apprentice held; he knew our reality is created based on the beliefs we hold. Yoda could see where his fear would take him based on his emotional state. His anger and fearful thoughts toward those who kept him from his mother would also determine if he would seek power from outside himself or from the force within. The young apprentice was formulating his identity around seeking outside power which could only lead to self-destructive reactions. My five-year-old son recited the Yoda speech in front of a college classroom explaining that fear and anger could lead to the dark side or negativity.

FEAR IS AN ENERGY SOURCE

Fear is the energy source for The Human Hamster Wheel which empowers the challenges to manifest in our lives. The struggle will continue if the fear is not replaced with another power source. The endless loop which can infect a family generationally can be stopped by one person in the chain who connects with another power source: the I AM. No matter what religious background you have there's no other way to come out of the darkness of fear and return to love than being connected to the source of that love. The alternative is found in the repetition of suffering.

FEAR CREATES CHAOS

Ego
From
Altering
Reality

FEAR IS LIKE A PRISM IT DISTORTS THE LIGHT.
We begin to see the world through the lens of our victimization

- Fear of not being Good enough
- Fear of Death
- Fear of failure
- Fear of being criticized

What fears keep you on the HUMAN HAMSTER WHEEL?

CREATING CHAOS

FEELINGS — POWER AND CONTROL REACTIONS — EVENTS — FEELINGS — POWER AND CONTROL REACTIONS — FEELINGS — EVENTS

FEAR

There are limited outcomes within the FEAR based thinking paradigm. In other words freedom and true choice do not exist.

Exercise Five

Take a moment to underline the fears in this chapter that create challenges in your life. Write in your "I AM" journal how they have affected you and where they came from. Remember that part of the healing process is the skill of being honest with yourself. Be honest when looking at the fears that present your biggest challenges. In The Human Hamster Wheel, add your fears to the diagram. This will help you understand the ego and the important role fear plays in our lives.

Reference

In this video I give two scenarios: 1) how hurt can turn into anger and 2) how hurt, when responded to with compassion, can dissipate. Knowing the alchemy of hurt can make us better lovers of humanity and can align us with the thoughts and actions of God.

In this video I give an example of the alchemy of hurt while teaching at the University of Nevada Las Vegas.
Video, "The Alchemy of Hurt" at drkarmen.com

CHAPTER SIX

POWER AND CONTROL REACTIONS (PCR)

"Your life is the fruit of your own doing. You have no one to blame but yourself."
~ Joseph Campbell

The purpose of our reactions is to avoid addressing our underlying fear. The power and control reaction on The Human Hamster Wheel gives the *illusion* of having power and control (PC). Remember, the trauma event causes us to feel helpless and powerless, therefore our reactions, which are chosen based on our feelings of helplessness and victimization, are an effort to get the power back. When there's a perception of victimization based on our fear triggers, the ego tries to avoid it by using the PC reactions. These are the first line of defense and can become our personality traits.

We identify with the ego seeking power and control as if this is who we are. But it's not who we are—it's merely the way we reacted when we perceived the original wound. The purpose of the PC reaction is to create a false sense of security. When the Power and Control Reactions (PCRs) are used, our world becomes limited by our fears. These fears are projected onto everything while we're unaware of the process. For example, my original wound happened in fifth grade when I developed a fear of being stupid or inferior. Every time a situation arose where I thought there could be a repeat of my wounding I would use my "go to" reactions:

- ☐ BLAME
- ☐ CRITICIZE/LIE
- ☐ MANIPULATE
- ☐ ARGUE/BULLY
- ☐ INTIMIDATE/THREATEN
- ☐ ISOLATE

These PCRs were developed within my ego to protect me from being wounded in the future. They're intended to gain power but there's an emptiness caused by the ever present wound. The ego keeps the fear and the wound intact because without those it can no longer exist. These reactions don't resolve or change anything but continue the pattern of victimization and suffering (HHW). The reactions give just enough of an illusion that we believe we're "WINNING".

Years ago a successful actor was fired from a television show due to his addictions and other out-of-control reactions. He launched a campaign that criticized and blamed the producers all the while touting that he was winning. Of course he wasn't winning; he was continuing his PCRs (Power and Control Reactions) which perpetuated his HHW (Human Hamster Wheel). What his story revealed is how determined his ego could stand even though his world was crumbling. The results of our ego are pointing us toward an inner solution, but we have to recognize that the hero's journey is inward. We can't hire a public relations firm to convince the world we're winning. The real work is when we recognize that the only way to win is by going to the wound that our ego uses drugs and money to avoid.

CRITICISM

The Internet provides ample opportunity for people to use criticism as a PCR. Cyber criticism is when someone posts an attack that criticizes someone's effort, whether it's an article, photo, performance, video or lecture. The comment might be a criticism filled with hate instead of constructive, encouraging thoughts. We can see this online or on TV talent shows that criticize the performer to the point of cruelty. The viewers tune in each week to see the uncomfortable embarrassment that's encouraged. The performer is in tears and the harshest comments bring good ratings.

We've created the term "Haters" for this relatively new phenomenon. Haters refer to those who don't do anything but criticize others who are doing something. Haters have taken criticism to the level of a spectator sport. They get a charge out of criticizing others and gaining a feeling of superiority. However, the charge is small and has to be repeated over and over to feel a sense of power and control. The hater has identified with their role of being critical and judgmental and incorporates this into their perceived personality. I once heard a famous performer say that when someone posts a negative comment online it's as if you're stopped at a traffic light and someone jumps in your car, cusses you out and jumps out. It can feel that assaultive. The anonymous nature of the Internet may increase the feelings of helplessness for the one being attacked. The hater meanwhile feels power when criticizing because they avoid their fear of being judged.

WHY DO WE CRITICIZE?

The person writing or saying hateful things is afraid of criticism. By inflicting it on others they can avoid their wound. Their outward attacks are a reflection of their fear of failure. When someone posts a hateful comment, they're revealing their wounds to the world. Outward displays of PCRs are meant to be a wakeup call to address the underlying fear. What we fear the most is what we'll act out in the world. Haters are slaves to their fear of being criticized and not being good enough. They connect to others by being critical, which keeps them unaware of the inner work needed for transformation.

THE EGO EXPOSED

The Power and Control Reactions are used by the ego personality which is always looking for ways to assert itself. Listen to your thoughts and notice that the ego is seeking power and control. It will look for a fight to resolve an imagined conflict. The delusional conflicts come from your ego's need for external power so it can be in control.

The ego will create a problem even when it doesn't exist. Its entire existence is built on avoiding our fears and wounding. Therefore the ego is hyper-vigilant looking for ways to protect itself when the danger is a delusion of its own creation. The ego remembers the original wounding with the help of the amygdala (which stores fearful memories). The ego thinks about how horrible that event was and how it was associated with an authority figure, therefore any authority figure may trigger the fearful thought which creates our reality. Thus when the reality shows up and triggers our PCRs, we're on The Human Hamster Wheel and are DELUSIONAL. The ego manufactures suffering as if it's a normal state of life, yet this is a delusion operating outside our conscious awareness.

The ego can come up with the PCR to the problem it made up and put it into action. This creates an unconscious running on the wheel which needs to be stopped consciously. Visualize a hamster running on the wheel: **we** know he's not going anywhere...but does **he?** When we unconsciously follow our ego and the fears it generates, we're not alive. We think we're accomplishing or solving something but we're just reacting instead of being responsive to our innermost self. Now visualize you're on the same Hamster Wheel living your life based on fears and false beliefs. The one observing you is your highest self, the soul or inner Hero. The soul knows you're not living or accomplishing anything....but the ego is a distraction from the truth.

LISTEN TO YOUR THOUGHTS AS AN OUTSIDE OBSERVER.

I truly believe that unless you listen to your thoughts as an outside observer, your ego will continue to stay unregulated. The ego goes unchecked because we're not fully conscious of its existence. It exists as long as you continue to be unaware that a better life is available without it. An awesome life waits just outside its range.

I left a five-year relationship and began the practice of observing my thoughts about the relationship. I felt as if I were a researcher objectively observing my subject. I was able to observe how my ego was interpreting the break up. It was trying to avoid the wound of not being good enough by feeling angry. My PCR was to blame my fiancé. My ego sat in judgment of his past action or inactions. For hours my thoughts ruminated about how wrong he was and how badly he treated me. My ego spent a lot of time going over different scenarios that never happened but if they had the tables would be turned and I would have power and control.

If I could take all the mental energy I used trying to change another person I could have cured cancer. This exercise was helpful and allowed me to see what my ego is capable of when left to its own devices. I increased my awareness by eavesdropping on my thoughts. Thoughts are powerful therefore I was finally able to see how the ego was creating my suffering. The ego's thoughts were strongest when it perceived me as a victim. And I came up with intentions for my fiancé that further victimized me. The more I became the victim in my mind the more I could make him the villain. The ego's way of reacting was to create a virtual world that seemed more difficult to escape. As the observer I knew I didn't want to live in that delusional world of protection at any cost. I didn't want to seek revenge, be bitter or refuse to fall in love again. I knew that there had to be a better way of living and it had to start with my thoughts. Whenever I caught my ego reflecting on my victimization, I would say, "NO that's not me!"

I was waking up. I was able to consciously switch channels getting my inner Hero's take on the break up. My inner Hero was able to see the situation from a higher vantage point. My thoughts were centered on my spiritual growth and how I had become too dependent on the relationship. I was looking for that other person to heal my fear of not being good enough. Instead I created an opportunity to heal that wound in the form of the relationship. I began to release all animosity and anger toward my fiancé by being my own hero in my own story. I felt an inner power when I held myself and my fiancé in loving and compassionate thoughts. The implementations of these thoughts were the polar opposite of the thoughts of the ego. By sowing the seeds of love instead of anger I could bring a harvest of abundance.

THE PCRS CAN ESCALATE THE AGGRESSION

The Power and Control Reactions can become increasingly aggressive and self-destructive based on the fears that developed around the time we formed our identity. While working in detention I interviewed teen inmates who committed aggressive acts. To the teens the assaults, pimping, selling drugs and burglary were normal acts based on their environment. Some were affiliated with gangs and lived in neighborhoods where aggression was survival—it was a normal part of going to elementary school and to the store in their neighborhood. The teens in detention had experienced the trauma and powerlessness that an aggressive environment taught. They formed their identity based on their exposure to these traumatic experiences. They identified and aligned themselves with gangs, weapons and overall aggressive tendencies to gain power. Some of the Power and Control Reactions common with aggression are:

- STEALING/ILLEGAL ACTIVITY
- DESTRUCTION OF PROPERTY
- ADDICTIONS
- INCARCERATION/RUNAWAY
- SELF-INFLICTED ABUSE
- ASSAULT/RAPE
- HOMICIDE/SUICIDE

These reactions are a symptom of the larger wound which is "not being enough". The teens continued to seek power in ever increasing ways of aggression but which never satiated the ego. Research indicates that video game exposure involving killing of human characters can be damaging to the human psyche and can contribute to expressing aggression at a young age. Exposure to aggression can be a way of gaining power and control even in a game form and can have an effect on young people's reaction to trauma. During the teen years we're formulating our identity and the aggression we're exposed to can directly influence our thoughts, feelings and behaviors. Police and military personnel are also vulnerable to these aggressive reactions because of their exposure to trauma where they're trained to take power and control in every situation.

SCHOOL SHOOTINGS

Everyone in America has heard of the Columbine school shootings in Colorado. Two teenage boys went to their high school highly armed and shot students randomly and targeted others. People were bewildered and confused as to how these upper middle class kids could do such an aggressive and violent act. The Human Hamster Wheel offers a tool to understand all PCRs. The boys used the ultimate form of power and control by committing suicide after their killing spree. Early adolescence is an important time in identity formation, because kids are developmentally at the stage where they separate from their parents and form their own self-concept. What they're exposed to in this particular stage of development is critical. Parents feel they have the right to scrutinize their children's friends knowing their peers have a big influence on them.

According to those who investigated the shooting at Columbine, the boys complained of being bullied from the popular cliques at school. They isolated themselves from other kids and formed their own clique. They were fans of violent video games which enforced revenge seeking PCRs. They identified with the characters in the video games and decided to carry out the ultimate form of bullying dressed in their role playing outfits.

In order to use the PCRs, a person has to feel powerless due to trauma. To seek power and control over others, the boys chose the behavior that would give them what they perceived was supreme power, like in the video game. By committing suicide the boys got the last word. They knew they couldn't be punished or criticized for their actions which would trigger the fear of not being good enough. The shooting was intended to avoid this wound and the suicide was their avoidance reaction. Suicide was the ultimate form of PCR to avoid the consequences of their actions, again like in a video game. In their ego state they racked up the most points without giving their opponent a chance to play.

WHY DO SUCH THINGS HAPPEN?

Sad to say, there have been many aggressive and violent acts in our country since Columbine. The media will continue to wonder why the person did it, stating we'll probably never know. I disagree—this is simply not the case. We do know why people do horrific acts: it's because they're seeking power and control over a situation or a person they feel utterly powerless over. They seek power and control in a way they think will give them respect, revenge and superiority. Their thoughts are limited to the aggressive reactions on The Human Hamster Wheel which gives them the illusion that they have no choice. I've heard many teens state that they didn't have a choice but had to hit the person or steal their car or commit whatever act for their survival. Their ego didn't offer another option because they were seeking external power. The ego doesn't offer choices, only limited reactions.

Whenever we react aggressively, we're avoiding the pain of our trauma by inflicting pain on others. We're no longer the *victim* but the *victimizer.* Joseph Campbell wrote: "Refusal of the summons converts the adventure into its negative. Walled in boredom, hard work, or 'culture,' the subject loses the power of significant affirmative action and becomes a victim to be saved. His flowering world becomes a wasteland of dry stones and his life feels meaningless—even though, like King Minos, he may through titanic effort succeed in building an empire or renown. Whatever house he builds, it will be a house of death: a labyrinth of cyclopean walls to hide from him his Minotaur. All he can do is create new problems for himself and await the gradual approach of his disintegration." (*The Hero with a Thousand Faces,* 1949)

By answering the hero's call, enlightenment will follow. When we understand that true power is gained from conquering our fearful thoughts and emotions, we're free from the ego-driven personality. We can now seek power from a new direction—instead of the outside in we view our Self from the inside out.

The Power and Control Reactions are mostly unconscious reactions to fear and the evidence of a spiritual void, which comes from our lack of knowing who we are. To activate or ignite our inner Hero we have to confront our fear instead of avoid it.

We are light beings. When we unconsciously react based on the impostor ego we perpetuate suffering. The Human Hamster Wheel can be used as a tool to help you decipher the ego's smoke screen. The ego has many fears and wants to keep them hidden so it can gain power and control based on The Human Hamster Wheel. The ego always reacts based on fear.

Exercise Six

Pay attention to your thoughts as if you're an outside observer. These thoughts interpret the past and fret over the future—and can be your inner critic. They're not you but you may think they are since they're happening in your head. Can you tell where the thoughts are coming from? Is it the ego or the soul (hero)? Write the Power and Control Reactions you use the most. Is this something you would like to change?

Reference

Our thoughts determine the meaning to any event or situation. When we master our thoughts and align them with the Divine, we see the world differently—through the lens of Gratitude, Love, Compassion and Acceptance. Remember, no matter the circumstance we can give it the meaning that has the highest vibration.
In this video I describe the process we can take to recognize that I AM the one who gives things meaning. This ability empowers us to choose how we see everything.
Video, "We Determine the Meaning" at drkarmen.com

CHAPTER SEVEN

FORGIVENESS

"Resentment is like drinking poison and then hoping it will kill your enemies."

~ Nelson Mandela

Before attempting to practice the Five Pointed Star I mentioned earlier, forgiveness is essential. It's a gift we give ourselves first. The anger and resentment of unforgiveness weighs us down and keeps us stuck on our Human Hamster Wheel. Visualize unforgiveness as two 100-pound weights tied around your waist. Then jump into the ocean; you'll sink despite your best efforts to swim. Suffering and struggling ensue when we do our best to change our outer circumstances without forgiving ourselves first. The higher consciousness can't fully be expressed if we're weighted with unforgiveness. When we forgive, especially those we've held long grudges against, we restore the connection to all things. Unforgiveness shuts us off from life and the infinite possibilities it holds for us. We accept limits on our life when we hold onto unforgiveness.

In the work environment I've heard coworkers express bitter, vengeful feelings about fellow employees. Even when the people no longer worked for the agency, the angry feelings remained over past perceived injustices. These harbored resentments affect our health, attitude at work and family relationships. The particular incident of perceived mistreatment may have happened years earlier but the brain can recall it as if it occurred yesterday. We can tell the suffering story with anger, frustration and venom which is stored in the memory centers of our brain. We give it extra meaning and long lasting power by believing it defined our identity. The reason the memory carried so much negative energy is that we became the negative experience. Every perceived slight triggered insecure feelings which had been there long before the person began working for the agency.

My insecurities would have been triggered if I worked for any company. I needed to have my negative emotions triggered in order to have an opportunity for spiritual growth. My Human Hamster Wheel was there to show me what needed to be changed in my thinking process. I was the leader of the "complaining group". I even organized lunches where we could all get together and discuss our victimization.

After practicing the Five Pointed Star for months, I could no longer participate in complaining with my coworkers. I had no need to carry the trauma files in my head. It was clear I was keeping a huge file cabinet of injustices that could easily be accessible. I would imagine the file cabinets in my office and didn't want to carry them around everywhere. They influenced my thoughts, feelings and actions in every situation, whether I was conscious of it or not.

HOW HEAVY IS YOUR FILE CABINET?

My coworker's story of victimization reminded me of conversations I had with my mother. I would complain about my "sperm donor" to anyone who would listen. Sperm Donor was the name I called my father; to his face I called him by his first name. I couldn't call him father or Dad because my file cabinet was full of reasons he didn't measure up to that label. I laid out my case like an attorney as to why my mother should leave him. I gave reasons why she should hate him like I did.

When I was listening to my coworker complaining, she used the skill set I honed as a teenager. I not only hated my father, I despised him. I blamed him for the trauma in my life. My feelings were no secret, as my entire family knew about my dark feelings toward him. When I was a teen, my mother asked me, "Why is it that every time your father walks into a room you walk out?" I wasn't aware this was happening. I could feel his energy and I instinctively removed myself from where he was. I was subconsciously trying to leave the negative energy behind. The toxic thoughts and feelings remained with me even when I left the room, the home and the state of Missouri.

I didn't understand that unforgiveness allowed the negative thoughts and feelings to remain within me and show up in my physical reality. I manifested situations and people in my life that represented the same characteristics I hated in my father. People who devalued, misjudged and betrayed me showed up in many forms. Bosses, coworkers and relationships were cast perfectly to trigger the negative emotions I never healed. Throughout my life these events would repeat until I was able to forgive the source of these feelings within myself.

WHY WE KEEP THE FILE

The file cabinet of unforgiveness may have some valid files in it. I'm not saying that the events didn't happen or that you don't have some true facts. We hold onto unforgiveness because we've been brainwashed to believe the lies that hating or holding onto resentment protects us. We believe that if we let go of the feelings of hatred we would be saying the behavior was acceptable. All these thought processes convince us that we're separate which makes it easier to fall into a pattern of unforgiveness. We believe we're separate from the person we hold resentment toward, which isn't the truth. We can then call them an enemy and label them in ways that distance us from them. We collect information for our file cabinet which attracts everything we don't want. While our ego collects evidence for our unforgiveness files, our soul wants us to return to forgiveness and love. The soul, or our highest self, wants us to take the experiences of suffering and recognize the opportunity to forgive ourselves and others.

MY FILE CABINET

I had a file marked "domestic violence" I'd kept since the age of three. My mother taught my sister and me how to dial the emergency number to call the police. She showed us how to put our finger in the O for operator and pull it in a circle around the dial of the telephone. The violent acts happened at night after we were in bed: a long evening of drinking, a short argument and then crashing violence. On one particular night I recall, my sister and I were asleep in our bunk beds and heard the banging of furniture. My mother screamed and I remember running to her room and seeing her mouth bloody as were the white sheets. Scared and confused, my sister who was a year older and I called the Operator who summoned the police. My mother went to the hospital and my father ran away before the police arrived. My sister and I went to our paternal grandparents' home until my mother was released. After that event my mother, who was in her late 20s, began wearing dentures because my father knocked out her front teeth. That incident would not be the end of the traumatic experiences that happened in our home.

I convey that story because I know about file cabinets and why we keep them. I kept my hatred for my father because I thought it provided me with safety and I could justify my feelings based on his behavior. I was going against my true nature of love so I had to consciously provide the reason for not forgiving. I kept putting reasons in my file cabinet why I couldn't forgive. I thought these reasons and feelings kept me safe from him and any other person who would come into my life to do me harm. That's how I justified my heart being closed. I withheld love, forgiveness and joy from my father not knowing that by doing so I kept it from myself. By withholding these attributes I couldn't manifest them in my life. I didn't come to realize until decades later that my feelings toward him were manifesting conflict at my job and in my relationships. I had moved thousands of miles away from him after high school and as an adult I was still unaware of how my current conflicts were connected to my unforgiveness toward my father.

YOU'RE RESPONSIBLE FOR CASTING THE PLAYERS IN YOUR LIFE

The Universe showed me, through a miraculous revelation, that my suffering was being caused by me! The Universe had been giving me opportunities to go within to change my self-concept to wholeness but due to unforgiveness it was a slow process. I needed to forgive the root of my conflict and get rid of the file cabinets reserved for my father because they reinforced my victim identity. I kept thinking people and events were doing things to me.

My victim thinking began when I was three and experienced the trauma of domestic violence which left me feeling helpless, terrified and confused. These feelings were not temporary; they were chronic and changed who I was born to be. I went through most of my life manifesting people and situations that would confirm my beliefs of victimhood. I was creating and re-creating my experiences based on who I thought I was…a victim, helpless and powerless. I'd hired myself to play a victim in my own movie and cast the other characters based on my role. Every victim needs a villain so I cast all the other characters in my movie as victimizers. No one does this consciously; I know I didn't.

MIRACLES OF MIRACLES

My miraculous experience happened in the late 1990s. I was on my way to work driving on the freeway. Instead of seeing the road in front of me I saw a vision of Jesus and a feeling of peace came over me. It felt as if I were a computer being downloaded with information. I woke up drenched in tears having no memory of parking my car, let alone getting off the freeway.

My overwhelming feeling was of **love.** I was shown through my senses how much my father was loved by God. I felt the love that surrounded him and this same love enveloped me. In that moment I was aware that there was one love for all and nothing could take it away. I learned that this love isn't based on behavior, so the file cabinet is useless. Love is based on your identity which is from the source. Negative behavior comes from fear which is not who we are. In the Bible it says: "We are not given a spirit of fear but of power and a sound mind."

A person's fear is not a reason to withhold love. When we withhold who we are (love) we go through life creating delusional experiences. I was also aware that God loved me and everyone else and that he doesn't love one more than the other. So I felt the love toward my father and the love he had for me at the same time. I never had a judgmental or unforgiving thought toward my father after that powerful experience. I loved him. I no longer judged him or held onto victim thoughts. On that day I was healed by that miraculous experience that helped me forgive everyone in my life. I wasn't getting along with my boss at work but after I experienced that cleansing miraculous vision, I loved him. After that experience I had compassion for my boss instead of anger.

Once I forgave or let go of my judgment, I could see that I had been the hero the whole time and didn't know it. I then began to embody non-judgment while being fully conscious. I saw the truth: **there are no villains**. I decided to consciously create a life filled with endless possibilities. I chose to think non-judgmentally, on purpose. My purpose was to be in the thoughts of the Creator. I was transformed by this miraculous experience and my relationship with my father was transformed. I began to see others with the love vision I received that day.

Compassion toward **those who haven't forgiven is key**. It took me a while to know that my bosses were my spiritual teachers. All my experiences of suffering at work and as a child were opportunities to reclaim my true identity. My bosses, coworkers and father all of whom I once thought of as enemies, turned out to be my shamans in disguise. All my experiences led me to acknowledge and ignite my inner Hero.

Was it a financial crisis or a wakeup call to greater abundance?

Forgiveness can free up the opportunity for abundance. The recession taught me a great deal about forgiveness. During the housing bubble, I bought my dream home like many Las Vegans. When the bubble burst in 2007 I owed more on my home than it was worth. During that same year I went through a divorce and had a serious car accident. Do you think the Universe was trying to give me opportunities to go within and return to love? I held anger toward my ex-husband, the recession and the bank that refused to refinance my home. I was angry with myself for getting into such a financial mess. These events offered an opportunity to let go of the harmful thoughts and feelings conjured up the cycle of suffering. I had to forgive myself for getting involved in a one-sided loan and ignoring the red flags that were all around me. I had to let go of the anger I felt toward the bank for not working with me. I had to transform my role as victim during the recession.

My home went into foreclosure which taught me that my identity is not found in material things. If I continued to see myself as a victim I would not be able to see the opportunity that came with the recession. If I had held onto the loss, anger and anguish I would have missed out on one of the best buying opportunities in my lifetime. Forgiveness boosted abundance; by letting go of the fear, anger and my victim story I was able to manifest everything I desired. I prospered while others were in crisis. Instead of being fearful of the real estate market based on my past experiences, I became excited at the opportunities that became visible.

"Forgiveness is letting go of the expectation that the past could have been any different."
~ Dr. Phil

MODELING FORGIVENESS

Forgiveness benefits everyone. My family and coworkers were affected when they observed the release of my resentment. When we forgive we can be fully present in the moment in all our conversations without projecting our stored up files onto our response. We then make decisions without the information from the file cabinet of past hurts. We then respond knowing what to say based on our inner Hero and not the ego that seeks power and control. With forgiveness we respond in the moment to each situation, based on who we are, not The Human Hamster Wheel. Forgiveness helps us be in the wisdom of the moment which is where truth and magic take place.

JUDGMENT

Judgment is the precursor to SEPARATION. In order for a person to forgive and let go of resentment and anger, the judgment that was formed needs to be released. We form anger and resentment based on a person we decided victimized us in some way. Learning to set our judgments aside and go straight to compassion when we see suffering puts us in the realm of the Kingdom of God. Retaining the CONNECTION takes practice; it's essential in the practice of being more like the light.

In order to be the light in the world, which is a directive in the Bible, we must be aware of the impulse to judge. The ego wants to be divisive by employing critical judgment in opposition of the way God thinks. Oneness becomes more real to us when we view others with compassion and love. When we judge others we separate them; a void is created when we're operating from the ego. Being non-judgmental takes practice. When we're non-judgmental we recognize that we're all from the same Divine source. Moment by moment practice this realization and you'll increase your identification with the Spirit in all.

I learned to be critical of others early, so being judgmental felt natural for me. I remember when my sister and I watched TV and heckled the performers. We judged everything about the performance and how the actors looked. Judgment became my way of viewing the world; I was critical of everything. So being non-judgmental doesn't come easy for me but I've learned how important it is in order to transform the cycle of suffering. When my ego tries to separate me from another person, I initialize compassion as a weapon against judgment.

PRACTICE BEING NON-JUDGMENTAL

The practice of non-judgment can be enlightening and can illuminate the ways we use judgments to feel safe. Judging has become a national pastime. *The Jerry Springer Show* and *American Idol* made judgment a cultural practice. Social media creates a medium for people to feel superior by judging.

When we think a person is less than, dumber or a bad person we've created dualism. Dualism and separation do not cultivate Oneness. Dualism is in opposition to the Kingdom of God. Thinking in this way is a reflection of the insecurity of the ego. When we react with judgments we focus on that limited description of our own delusion. Our interactions with those we've judged is distorted and convoluted. True communion can only be accomplished beyond insecurities that hinder Oneness. The more separate we are from living things, the more aggressive the impulses we have. Judgment is based on fear and doesn't operate on the same vibration as universal consciousness.

WHAT DO THE SCRIPTURES SAY ABOUT FORGIVENESS?

Forgiveness is mentioned in all world religions. In the New Testament Jesus embodied forgiveness. In his journey he showed us how to put forgiveness into practice. Jesus loved people even though he knew they would betray him. He practiced compassion toward those who were victims of their own thinking. He implemented compassion automatically because he knew that their behavior had everything to do with their spiritual growth and nothing to do with his identity. In other words, he didn't take their actions personally. They didn't *know* him because they didn't know who they were.

He showed compassion toward others whom society had shunned or judged harshly. His words and actions showed that he wasn't judging them but he was able to understand them and love them. In the Bible there's an example of a woman who was about to be stoned by a large crowd for committing adultery. Jesus entered the circle and standing with the woman he said, "He who has not sinned throw the first stone." The crowd dispersed without a single stone being thrown. Jesus knew that to condemn and judge the woman so harshly they were ashamed of their own acts. When we withhold forgiveness from ourselves, we can't give it to someone else. How we treat someone is an indication of how we view ourselves. The truth is we're all One and the lie is separation.

Jesus didn't have a file cabinet full of reasons he shouldn't like or trust another person. His inner vision allowed him to see through to the core of that person and recognize their identity as his own. When a person acted in a way that conveyed they didn't recognize who they were, Jesus could discern the truth of their identity. He treated each person based on the truth instead of their outward demonstration. He responded to people with love and compassion because he was love and compassion. The Bible makes it clear that embodiment of the Divine can happen by being the attributes of that presence. The presence within you doesn't judge, therefore it doesn't need to forgive. When we find we haven't forgiven someone, when we do, it aligns us with the Kingdom of God. Our heart is receptive to hear the voice of the Divine within us. We can then attract more freely the highest expression of ourselves.

> *"Therefore, if you are offering your gift at the altar and there remember that your brother or sister has something against you, leave your gift there in front of*

> *the altar. First go and be reconciled to them your brother; then come and offer your gift."*
> ~ Matthew 5;23-24

Jesus talked about the importance of forgiveness throughout his ministry. He spoke about it in the midst of the betrayal and crucifixion. It's written that he said, "Father forgive them for they know not what they do." He knew those who didn't understand him were perpetuating their cycle of suffering which could remain with them for generations. The only way to break the cycle was to recognize the Christ Consciousness within, and by doing so recognize it in everyone. Those who persecuted Jesus didn't recognize themselves in him. He was viewed as an enemy instead of the invitation to return to love. Jesus recognized everyone as the I AM presence. He had access to the Kingdom of God which gave him the power to love and show compassion when it was most difficult. He taught that the Kingdom of Heaven is here and now and everyone can have access to it.

Instead we go through life using our own perception to justify our mistakes, our anger, our impulses to attack or our lack of love in whatever form it may take. We see a world of evil, destruction, malice, envy and despair. All this we must learn to forgive; not because we're "good" and "charitable" but because what we're seeing isn't true. We've distorted the world by our twisted defenses and are therefore seeing what is not there. As we learn to recognize our perceptional errors, we forgive ourselves, looking past our distorted self-concepts to the Self. We are then about to recognize what God created in us and it can be expressed fully as us.

EXPERIENCE OF FORGIVENESS

When I experienced the miraculous insight of how God viewed my father, it opened my awareness. The awesome experience taught me that we can understand how much we're all loved and can feel this love in our everyday life. We don't have to wait until we feel love envelop us; we can instead feel the vibration from within. We can feel the love envelop us as we see in our mind's eye that love is us. Fill your senses with this love toward yourself and expand it to others.

Exercise Seven

Forgive those who trigger you because they're showing you what needs to be healed within you. When we let go of the anger and resentment, we gain more light energy from the source. It's time to release the anger and look at the fear that tries to hold it in place. Identify the fear based on the list of fears in a previous chapter. Do the work that's needed to go to the next level of knowing your true identity. When we release the anger which is projected as inner fear, we can more clearly see that we're the person forgiving and the one forgiven. Therefore when we activate this inner vision through forgiveness we heal ourselves.

Reference

I can't emphasize enough the importance of forgiveness on the path to spiritual growth. It's crucial if our goal is to align with the mind of God. In order to eliminate fear we must forgive the perceived slights, attacks, mistakes or acts done from the ego. Our life can do a radical 180 degree turn when we let go of the egoic emotions by forgiving.

In this video you'll hear about my transformation when I forgave my father.

Video, "The Power of Forgiveness" at drkarmen.com

CHAPTER EIGHT

THE CONNECTION

"You may believe that you are responsible for what you do, but not for what you think. The truth is that you are responsible for what you think, because it is only at this level that you can exercise choice. What you do comes from what you think."
~ Marianne Williamson, author of <u>A Return to Love: Reflections on the Principles of A Course in Miracles"</u>

In order to gain clarity about Oneness, *The Course in Miracles*, which is a course in how to connect with God, focuses on the real and unreal between knowledge and perception. The Course explains that what God creates is real and lasting and what the ego projects are our perceptions which are delusional. The world of perception is how we see the world based on our trauma and victim experiences. Conflict and competition based on lack and loss infiltrate our point of view, while judgment fuels our relationships. When you know the mind of God, you know nothing is separate from God because his creation shares one intention. In order to achieve the mind or intentions of the Creator, fear is transformed with perfect lessons in forgiveness. Each time we discover ways to forgive, love, accept and show compassion toward ourselves and others we awake from the dream world. The ultimate gift to be received by this knowledge is the reconciliation of the seeming opposites on which this world is based. What once seemed like an injustice done to one by someone else now becomes a call for compassion and union. When we view life in this way we have transformed Fear back to Love.

"The Truth shall set you free."
~ Jesus

What is the truth? The truth is that we create our reality with our fear-based thoughts. All the events in our life are there to return us to God, the vibration of love. Love is all there is. The return to love is a journey that's created based on your individual spiritual path to higher consciousness. It won't look like anyone else's because it will be tailor made by you.

When a traumatic event happens there's always the opportunity to change the thought from helpless victim to powerful Creator. Thereby you're breaking the ego and establishing a different paradigm which is the spiritual awakening process. It's characterized by a change of thought that your authentic power is within you and can't be taken away.

By practicing **Trust, Compassion, Gratitude, Acceptance and Love**, we exercise the muscles of the hero within. Fear dissipates as we return to our authentic loving nature When these five practices are utilized instead of the PCRs, the suffering is replaced by empowering thoughts. With repeated practice our brain is rewired to re-form our life with our new intentional thought. The Hamster Wheel is no longer generated by our fear and we ignite our inner Hero who has been waiting for our intentions to match a higher vibrational frequency.

GIVER OF LIGHT: CREATOR SOURCE PRESENCE

Throughout this book you may have noticed that I AM using several words to reference God. I may use Universe, energy, presence and Christ Consciousness or refer to the attributes of God as Power, Creativity and Love. All these are ways to describe the indescribable nature of God. The light energy is neither masculine nor feminine, neither solid nor invisible: the Divine Mother responsible for the birth of creation and the Divine Father of protection. There's no one word that can conjure up the magnificence of the One who created us in its image. When we put a label on this energy we limit who we are. Recognize the many faces of God in all the ways this energy is revealed, including your own mirror. The Brahman/ Spirit/ Light is what and who you are. The I AM is whatever you need it to be, dictated by that moment. Know that the hero within you is fearfully and wonderfully made for your special individual journey.

> *"You create intimacy when you shift from the pursuit of external power (ability to manipulate and control) to the pursuit of authentic power, the alignment of our personality with the Soul."*
> ~ Gary Zukav and Linda Frances, authors of *Seat of the Soul*

BEING

Being is when we become the essence of who we are. We embody Love, Compassion, Acceptance, Trust and Gratitude. In our daily life we become more of who we are until it's all we see. We are the solution and the manifestation of abundance shows up because we allow it. A sign of spiritual maturity is when we see the world as we are: loving, accepting and compassionate.

The ultimate truth and good news is that we are the manifestation of GOD. When we really get this truth, there's a paradigm shift that can rock our world. I grew up with a concept of God that was outside of me and now I AM talking about God being within me. It used to hurt my brain to think about how different this was from the way I was raised. I grew up in a church that was very formal with bishops, conferences and a God that was sitting on a throne in Heaven. I've been to churches where a sculpture of a bleeding Jesus on the cross was at the center of the altar. These images didn't connect with me as a child. It didn't make sense that I was praying for things from an image on a cross or a white bearded man in the clouds.

What does make sense is that spirituality goes beyond images and doctrine to unveil a closer connection to the God of the Universe. This Creator of all things made me with the same attributes that were used in the creation of the Universe. The Bible talks about man being made in God's image. The image of God isn't made up of facial features but of the energy of creative power or LIGHT.

The love I've experienced from this energy is personal and unifying. What makes sense to me is that the God of the Universe is closer than my neck vein and in my deepest breath. When we connect with this energy we're able to change our lives and be proactive in creating our reality.

DIVINE EMBODIMENT

Jesus is one of the best teachers of the embodiment of the Divine. Jesus said, "The Father and I are One. If you see me, you see the One who sent me." This was seen as blasphemy to organized religion. The religious counsels in the time of Jesus made their living and fed their egos by perpetuating the concept of a separate, judgmental God. In order to get a blessing from God, people believed they had to buy a sacrificial animal at the temple and have the priests perform a ritual of purification. As long as the people felt condemned by God they fed the coffers of the religious counsel.

When Jesus came to the temple he could see how distorted this charade was and he condemned this practice. He taught that there was no need for a middle man because God is within all of us. He taught of a loving and compassionate entity who wanted them to have abundance. Jesus became a threat to the counsel because they were afraid of losing their authority and financial stream. He was the enemy of the status quo. They rejected him because he was modeling an inner connection to God. Jesus said, "I AM the way, the truth, and the light." The way Jesus was living was the way of God. He put his ego aside and aligned with the thoughts of God and was led by this higher consciousness or Kingdom intentions.

Jesus responded with love and compassion which he taught was the way to end the cycle of suffering. He didn't identify himself as a victim even when he was hung on a cross next to the thieves and murderers. It's intentionally stated in the Bible that he freely gave his physical body though it had little to do with his mission of turning people away from Fear back to Love. By following the Kingdom consciousness, physical matter loses its priority because it's strongly attached to the ego. Jesus was aligned with the creative energy co-creating with his physical body until it was no longer of use. Jesus, the Divine Spirit, taught many of his important metaphysical lessons without the physical body. He instructed his disciples to BE THE ONE or to listen to the one wisdom inside them. The hero's journey can only be seen, interpreted and fully experienced in the metaphysical realm where time, space and the five senses cease to have control over meaning. When this happens your very being is lost in the source of all things and you are One.

We have been given the creative power to manifest our desires using this energy. Our thoughts and feelings are energy we use to create our physical world. We are all One which means we're all made up of this light energy.

PRESENCE

I had a glorious experience while in an airport surrounded by hundreds of people rushing and waiting for their plane. I sensed and knew I was surrounded by God. I loved everyone and saw that they were not their individual personalities but were all One energy. They were beautiful beams of light. I almost missed my flight because I wanted to hug everyone and tell them life was great. I wanted them to know they were beautiful. Words could not express the beauty I felt, so I cried. I was grateful I could see it and wanted it to last; it didn't, but I AM grateful for the glimpse.

We see the outward expression of Oneness when we're open to the truth. The expression of the Divine can be seen in a tree, a person at the checkout line and those surrounding you in an airport. There's no escaping the visuals that are everywhere all the time. The sunset is a sign of the creativity and the news on TV is a reminder to return to love. Everywhere is a reminder of the One.

We participate in the dance of the Divine with every breath we take. We generate the light of the Creator by being all the attributes of the energetic love vibration of the Universe. In order for us to say to everyone we meet

"Namaste", which means I honor the Spirit in you that is also in me, we have to recognize it in ourselves first.

Exercise Eight

Do you have a practice that allows you to feel more connected to the Universe? Are there times in your life or moments in your day when you feel the presence of God? Then take more time to do this practice and spend more moments feeling the presence. If not, find ways to make the connection to your source.

Reference

Whether you use the word God, Universe, Light or Energy it makes no difference. Whatever you call this Divine source it's important to have a connection or relationship to it.

In this video I explore the connection and the visuals that can help us to form this bond.

Video, "The Universe and You, an Awesome Connection" at drkarmen.com

CHAPTER NINE

THE FIVE POINTED STAR

"Congratulations to the one who came into being before coming into being.
If you become my disciples and pay attention to my sayings, these stones will serve you.
For there are five trees in Paradise for you; they do not change, summer or winter,
and their leaves do not fall. Whoever knows them will not taste death."
~ Gospel of Thomas 1:19

The five practices I've developed, called the Five Pointed Star, can help rewire the brain to accommodate and accept the identity of your inner Hero. I practice them in each moment and they keep me immune to the cycle of suffering. The Five Pointed Star provides a simple framework of how to consciously create from Love, Gratitude, Compassion, Acceptance and Trust, instead of creating from fear and the need for power and control.

While working with families conducting in-home therapy, I was supposed to tell the families to stop watching television. My supervisor believed the TV shows and the amount of time playing video games were to blame for the aggression that was being exhibited. I asked her what they should replace it with. She seemed puzzled. I explained that in order to get rid of one behavior or way of living your life, you have to put something in the void. When I started a low carb diet, for example, I replaced sugar, flour, rice and pasta with foods that didn't contain these items. But to ask someone to stop doing something without offering a replacement would increase the probability that the habitual behavior would continue.

WHAT DO I REPLACE THE HUMAN HAMSTER WHEEL OF SUFFERING (EGO) WITH?

When we want to change the pattern of The Human Hamster Wheel we need to replace it with the Five Pointed Star. This is an easy way to ask ourselves if we're generating the light and it offers a visual reminder of five practices to ignite your inner Hero.

> *"The light shines in the darkness, and the darkness can never extinguish it."*
> ~ John 1-5 (NLT)

When we incorporate the Five Pointed Star into our daily practice of being the light, there will be an expansion of creative inspiration and endless possibilities. You can manifest everything that will facilitate your hero's purpose.

As we come together with this new way of viewing the world (higher consciousness), we reap the benefits of a kinder, more abundant reality of our own creation: a world that doesn't see itself as separate from the environment or people. Separation and helplessness keep the cycle of suffering turning and creating predictable patterns in a limited expression of Self. Connection to the source is the birth of the manifestation of everything we desire. When we implement the five practices we transform Fear back into Love. The helpless feeling from our past conditioning dissipates and what remains is the inner Hero ready to take the ego's place. The hero's power comes from the inner light energy that the Five Pointed Star releases.

The five practices to ignite the inner Hero are:

LOVE: Yourself first; only then can you share it
COMPASSION: Non-judgment/ Empathy
ACCEPTANCE: Forgiveness/ Surrender
GRATITUDE: Thankful for the challenges and life
TRUST: Knowing everything is going to be okay

These five practices are the key to recalling your dependence on outside circumstances to change. Instead you have the power within you to transform the outer manifestation. These practices when used regularly will replace conditioned fear reactions to your real Self: a powerful, dynamic, compassionate and creative hero. We are the creative artists of life painting how we see the world AS it really is. We now use the paint brush to capture the Creator's intentions of love.

LEARNING A NEW WAY OF BEING

The Five Pointed Star practices, when used repeatedly, can reframe your belief system, change your thoughts and rewire your brain. In college my major was mental health research with an emphasis on how we learn and process information. Let's take the letters of the alphabet, for example: through constant repetition we learn random nonsensical shapes. The teacher told us to sing the ABC song knowing we would learn the order of the letters. We traced the lines that formed the shape of each letter over and over again. Through these practices we learned how to communicate by writing complex symbols. The meaning of the symbols came later when we associated the letters with everyday visuals, like C for CAT. We take these complex skills for granted and don't appreciate the amount of practice that was involved. The skill of reading and writing couldn't be accomplished without practice. In order to learn any skill there must be a willingness and openness to the learning process. To expand our consciousness, vibrate at a higher frequency and increase our awareness it takes practice.

"Instead, let the Spirit renew your thoughts and attitudes."
~ Ephesians 4:23 (NLT)

CHANGING THE WAY WE THINK

When I was in graduate school the professor told us we were being trained to think like social workers. I didn't realize what that meant until I was talking to other professionals. I was amazed at how different my thought process was from theirs. I had to give extra explanation about how I perceived a situation and why. My opinion was based on my education and field experience and their solutions came from their training. Probation officers viewed the world through a criminal justice lens while the attorney's perspective was based on the law. You may have examples of how you were taught a world view that changed the way you think.

The five practices are intended to change the way we see everything. When we implement these practices we can navigate through life differently. We'll be able to see opportunity where others see obstacles. We no longer have boundaries or limitations because our inner Hero doesn't believe they exist.

One of my favorite Bible verses reveals the truth about an expansion of consciousness.
> "But seek ye first the kingdom of God, and his righteousness;
> and all these things shall be added unto you."
> ~ Matthew 6-33

Instead of trying to manipulate the outside world to get external power and control, we begin to search for our true inner identity. When we create based on our authentic being then we tap into the Kingdom of God where *intention creates reality*. Everything is to be found in who and what we are and our identity can only be found in the Kingdom of GOD (higher consciousness). We are the hero we seek.

WHAT IS THE KINGDOM OF HEAVEN/GOD?

The five practices are a way to increase our view of the endless possibilities the Kingdom of God holds. Expand your way of thinking so the Kingdom of Heaven isn't a place you go when you die but a place that gives you life now. Think of the Kingdom of God as a head space that creates Heaven on Earth. By embodying this way of being, the energy generated creates an imaginative and purposeful life. The Kingdom of God is a way of participating in the world through connection rather than separation. Authentic power replaces helplessness and repetitive dysfunctional patterns. Imagination is a tool children use to access a world that's limitless. They imagine they can fly and the world stands as an awe inspiring adventure. Yet, school, adults and our culture may devalue this gift pointing out the rationale to shut it down. We leave behind the wonder, curiosity and adventure and replace it with fear. Our imagination is a gift from our Creator and a road map to finding our way back to love.

If we could imagine a world without war, abuse and suffering then it's achievable. If we only believe in the chaos we see then we'll continue to perpetuate suffering. Imagine as John Lennon said a world without conflict and the world will live as One. Martin Luther King had a dream where everyone lived in harmony. He knew with his spiritual knowledge that the vision begins by seeing what is not present in the physical. When we share these imagined visions it will become reality in the physical world.

Imagine what your life would be like if you practiced the Five Pointed Star. What kind of hero could you be? The five practices can be implemented at any time and in every moment. Incorporate them into your life and share the path with others based on your inner guidance.

The Five Pointed Star

LOVE

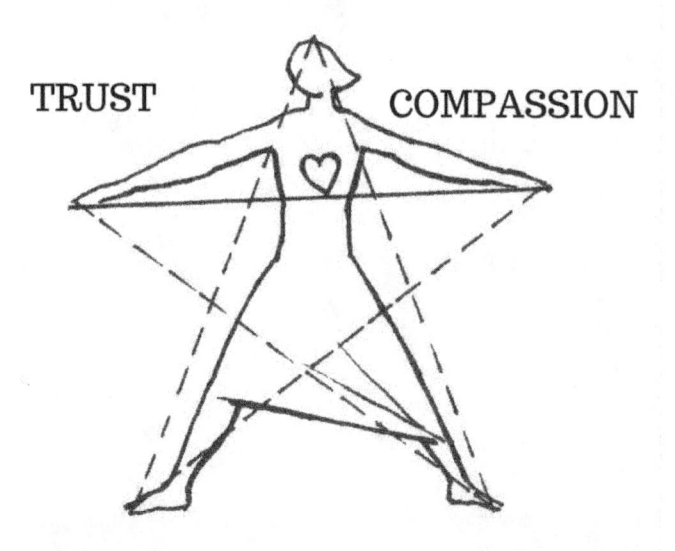

TRUST   COMPASSION

ACCEPTANCE   GRATATUDE

TOP OF THE STAR: LOVE

The top of the Five Pointed Star is Love, which according to the Bible is the most important practice. View everything with love. When we're confronted with someone with different views or even persecutors, our response should be conceived with love and compassion. The intention or point is to allow love to be the response to each situation and person. God is Love, therefore your main purpose in life is to be **Love**.

2ND POINT OF LIGHT: COMPASSION

The next point on the star is the practice of Compassion. Compassion is a moment-to-moment practice where we have concern for the sufferings or misfortunes of others. It's the response you give when you're confronted with a person who's stuck on The Human Hamster Wheel and views themselves as a victim. You're filled with empathic feelings toward them, sharing their pain and shining the light of love and understanding. The evidence of suffering must always initiate the response of compassion. The Intention/point to Compassion is to initiate the feeling of Oneness instead of judgment. Showing compassion to ourselves first, will allow us to freely give it to others. When we show compassion as the response to hurt, healing will follow.

3RD POINT OF LIGHT: GRATITUDE

The next point on the star is the practice of Gratitude. Our natural state of being is to be grateful for everything in our life. So this practice when done consistently is as natural as breathing. No matter what's going on outwardly we have much to be thankful for. Being grateful for the beautiful day, for the next breath, for the people in our life—these are all opportunities to express gratitude. If being grateful is a foreign concept for you then getting in the habit of saying all you're thankful for is essential. Gratitude extended to our past and present situation miraculously changes our perception. We begin to change our brains wiring to see the good and expect that good will come from the event.

4TH POINT OF LIGHT: ACCEPTANCE

Acceptance can take on several different twists and turns. Basically it means that we accept responsibility for our lives instead of blaming others for our fate. It's accepting instead of avoiding our fears which is how we create the experiences for suffering. Accepting our awesome attributes instead of the false limited identity leads to the end of suffering. Accept that there's another way of thinking and being as a daily practice. Allow miracles into your life by accepting that they are all around us waiting for our vision to expand. When we expand our field of perception we can see what has been there the whole time, perfection. Accept that the Universe is full of miracles and magic.

5TH POINT OF LIGHT: TRUST

Trust that the Creator desires your highest good. Knowing that all things are working together for your good is comforting. The Bible and other spiritual texts refer to the intentions of God: "I know the plans I have for you to prosper you and protect you." "I came so that you can have life more abundantly." We've been told that the intention of GOD is not to harm you or have you suffer, but to provide and protect you. Trust that you have everything you need inside of you for any challenge. You are more than enough, just know that. When you know and trust the power within you, your actions will be fearless. We need to trust this is true and happening right now.

THE GOAL OF THE FIVE POINTED STAR IS TO ATTAIN CONNECTION WITH THE MIND OF GOD.

THE UPANISHADS

The Upanishads refer to the secret teachings that were written in Sanskrit. No one knows who wrote them or when. The sages, saints and seers wrote their experiences of the Brahman or God presence. They recorded these sacred texts called Upanishads which translates as "sitting near devotedly". The sages must have felt like devoted students sitting at the feet of the Universal energy listening and visualizing the story of creation and then writing about their experiences.

The Upanishads illustrates the role of the Creator and our role within creation. *"The Imperishable is the Real. As sparks innumerable fly upward from a blazing fire, so from the depths of the Imperishable arise all things. To the depths of the Imperishable they in turn descend....Self-luminous is that being and formless. He dwells within all and without all...He is the innermost self of all."* Mundaka,II.i.1-4.

"Self illuminosity is Brahman (God), ever present in the heart of all. He is the refuge of all, he is the supreme goal. In him exists all that moves and breathes. In him exists all that is. He is both that which is gross and that which is subtle. Adorable is he. Beyond the ken of the senses is he. Supreme is he. Attain thou him.... He is the principle of life. He is speech, and he is mind. He is real. He is immortal. Attain him, O my friend, the one goal to be attained!" Ibid.,ii.1-2.

Exercise Nine

The Five Pointed Star is more important than The Human Hamster Wheel. It's essential to know how to disclose the ego for what it is—"fear"—and it's crucial to connect with the heart and intentions of God. Take a few moments and ask yourself how you can implement the Five Pointed Star in a situation at work or with your family. How can you be more Loving, Compassionate, Grateful, Accepting and Trusting toward everyone in your life? Trust that to see positive changes, inner forgiveness is the spiritual key to releasing the hold of the ego.

Reference
The Five Pointed Star has been crucial in keeping the light of the Creator flowing in my life. I have used it with children with encouraging results. It's easy to remember because the Five Pointed Star is symbolized by our body, so include it in your spiritual practice. Let me know if this is helpful to you.

In this video I give a brief description of the Five Pointed Star. Video, "The Five Pointed Star" at drkarmen.com

In the next five chapters we'll practice the Five Pointed Star and generate more Light with Love, Compassion, Gratitude, Acceptance and Trust. Being the I AM is when we become the essence of who we are. We embody Love, Compassion, Gratitude, Acceptance and Trust. In our daily life we become more of who we are until it's all we see. We are the solution, and the manifestation of abundance shows up because we allow it. A sign of spiritual maturity is when we see the world as we are: loving, accepting and compassionate.

CHAPTER TEN

PRACTICE LOVE

"Love everybody. Love when it's hard to Love. Our loving will change the World."

~ Ricki Byers Beckwith

Love is the outpouring of our essence. It comes from the core of who we are. When we ignite our inner Hero we experience love freely. In the past we may have been concerned about what others thought so we resisted a loving gesture. We may have been afraid of judgment or other negative consequences so we squelched our loving impulses. When we're no longer bound by our fear we're free to share and experience more love in our life.

In western culture romantic love gets all the attention. We see romantic movies and come to believe that this display of love is what defines the word. Few stories are shown that don't depict sexual or romantic love. The love expressed within our soul is the greatest love story we can experience. The soul or inner Hero loves you despite your behavior. Your inner Hero is your God Self and is timeless. It never dies or sleeps. Your hero sees everything and always wants your highest good. We yearn to be fully present in this love.

When we perceive the disconnect or separation of this love we turn to outside sources to feel loved. Alcohol, drugs, shopping, eating, gambling and sex will never fill the empty hole that's felt when inner love and joy isn't recognized. Our soul, the spiritual presence of God, is conspiring for our good through the pure love it expresses through us. If we're not aware of this love we're not fully alive. We continue to seek our essence in outside experiences and things. Meanwhile within is a wellspring of everything. The love within is like a fountain of unlimited water able to give us what we need in any given moment.

INNER LOVE

True Love is an intimacy that provides a connection with all things. This love provides security because it can never disappear. Love provides inspiration and creativity that's unique and continuous. This love is unconditional and doesn't judge or condemn but is joyful that we exist. When we're connected to this love we begin to see others through a lens of love which delights even when people aren't behaving in a way that's for their highest good. Even if someone is acting in a destructive manner, our response is compassion which is a loving practice. When it's hard to love, love anyway. When we transform our response from fear to love, we change the world. Love not based on circumstances but on who we are is powerful. Ancient spiritual teachers taught the practice of AGAPE: unconditional love.

The love our inner Hero has for us is that of a loving teacher. The spiritual teacher from India, Paramahansa Yogananda, shared an experience he had after running away and then returning to his spiritual teacher in the ashram. "Even though I ran away, his love for me remained unchanged. He didn't rebuke me. He said, 'If my love can be bribed to compromise itself, then it is not love. If I have to alter my behavior toward you for fear of your reaction, then my feeling for you is not true love. I must be able to speak to you honestly. You can walk out anytime, but so long as you are with me I will remind you, for your highest good, when you miss the mark.'" Yogananda went on to say, "I had never imagined anyone could be so interested in me. He loved me for myself. He wanted perfection for me. He wanted me to be supremely happy. That was his happiness. He wanted me to know God; to be the Divine for whom my heart longed."

LOVE IS A NOUN AND A VERB

A few years ago I wrote a foreword to a book about grief and loss. In it I wrote, "We are love." When the book was published I received a copy and what I wrote was changed to "We are loved." The author must have thought it was a typo but I was using the word love as a noun. Love is who we are and identifies us. From our identity come our thoughts, feelings, actions and results. Our identity is based on Love, Compassion, Gratitude, Acceptance and Trust. From this practice of the Five Pointed Star we'll find peace, forgiveness, power, joy and wholeness. We love people not based on their behavior but because that's who we are—love. We are love itself. By expressing love to ourselves and the source we unlock the collective soul.

> *"Love heals, renews, inspires and empowers us to do great things.*
> *Makes us feel safe and brings us closer to God."*
>
> ~ Deepak Chopra

It's imperative that we love ourselves first. By being love we manifest it in the physical. By being love, love will show up. You've heard the saying: "You have to love yourself first before you can love another". The spiritual Universe can't give you something you don't believe. By believing your true identity is love, you can be love to others. The love from within is coiled within our DNA but we must know how to access it. Love is not something we need to search for or pine for. Unconditional agape love is what we're born with. Agape doesn't judge but shows compassion for our Self and all things. History labels agape lovers as saints, messiahs and martyrs.

RADICAL AGAPE LOVERS

Nelson Mandela was imprisoned for 28 years because he opposed apartheid. Instead of hating his guards or the ones who put him there, he forgave and showed compassion. People were astonished that he came out of prison free of anger and hate. He didn't organize to kill his oppressors as some thought might happen. He instead instituted ways for the country to release the pain of the past years of oppression. He led others to respond with compassion by showing them what it looked like. He and Bishop Desman Tutu taught people how to release years of resentment and anger. Nelson Mandela had forgiven while in prison—not the day he was released. He had laid the groundwork of love that would change the world. He was a person who saw through the lens of love which was the catalyst for change.

He became the president of South Africa. He knew he needed to align with the value that could not support apartheid: love. He and his fellow prison mates knew they couldn't change a system using the same mental process that held it in place. They cultivated within themselves agape resulting in Oneness instead of separation. Agape love views others as Self. Judgment and separation are the opposite of what would create connection. Agape love sees the connection with others and that causing hurt would perpetuate the cycle of suffering. Nelson Mandela included the population that instigated apartheid in the change process knowing that lasting change could not be built on separation. He became a unifying force reminding us what we're capable of when we see only One.

Gandhi was the inspiration for the non-violent civil rights movement in the United States. Dr. Martin Luther King Jr. said about Gandhi's revolution of British occupied India: "He used love as a social and political force for change." Dr. King, Gandhi, Mother Theresa and Jesus are all examples of "Radical Lovers". When we see through the eyes of Oneness we'll appear different to those who see separation. Radical lovers will stand out like aliens in a strange world. The radical lovers appear limitless and fearless when revealing the truth.

There have always been teachers of Divine Love but now it's time to be the lessons they came to teach. We have infinite potential at our fingertips; our inner Hero is ready to activate the greatness that we are. Our inner Hero can visualize the infinite possibilities while others see danger and chaos.

YOU ARE A RADICAL LOVER

Radical lovers have mountain top experiences that guide them forward. Instead of surrendering to fear, doubt and disbelief a radical lover chooses love. A mountain top experience is when we view the endless possibilities through the mind of God. We all have access to the Kingdom through love which holds this magnificent viewfinder. The world can present with a critical and limited view but the God consciousness presents with a higher overview that dissolves limitation and restriction. Love opens the Kingdom of God and an outpouring of all we believe is possible. Radical lovers are visionaries knowing who they are and that through love all things are manifested and brought to life. Radical lovers access a love that surpasses human understanding of what's possible. They called forth the attributes of the Five Pointed Star to transform Fear back to Love. The space they held allowed for change to spring forth through conscious creativity.

"Let's make the impossible so very possible by loving. Love is the key."

~ Stevie Wonder

CONSCIOUS CREATIVITY

We can all consciously create by believing our hero is within us. By being the Five Pointed Star, we'll experience The Kingdom of Heaven on Earth. Jesus made the connection between our attributes matching God's attributes when he said, "But I tell you, love your enemies and pray for those who persecute you, that you may be children of your Father in heaven. He causes his sun to rise on the evil and the good, and sends rain on the righteous and the unrighteous. If you love those who love you, what reward will you get? Are not even the tax collectors doing that? And if you greet only your own people, what are you doing more than others? Do not even pagans do that? Be perfect, therefore, as your heavenly Father is perfect." Matthew 5:44-48

Jesus conveyed to those who had ears to hear: "The Father and I are One". John 10:30

This means: Be love and there will be no separation between you and the Father. The Father and you are One when you begin to match the spiritual vibration of the Creator.

LOOKING FOR LOVE IN ALL THE WRONG PLACES

I reconnected with a dear friend recently. I hadn't seen him in eight years and we hadn't had a heart-to-heart in at least 12. When we were catching up after so many years, he described from his perspective the relationships I had been in. As he spoke I realized I must have been a drama queen. I remember thinking, Wow, Yes, I remember that but that's so not who I

AM now. I must have been a heavy emotional energy burden to him as a friend. It was good to be reminded of how far I'd come and that I don't want to go back to that old identity.

My past history with relationships was drama filled and painful. I needed relationships to fulfill my neediness. When those relationships didn't make me feel safe, I was afraid, angry and upset with myself and the other person. I had assigned my relationship partners to be my saviors. I was like a bottomless pit and expected others to provide me with what I thought I needed. I was setting myself up for the inevitable which is to be a victim. The balloon had to burst but I didn't know it when I was blowing it up. Sometimes, though, I knew the relationship was doomed.

My soul was showing me through my experiences that I AM the love and security I was looking for in others. I AM everything I need to fill my hole. I needed to turn to the love within me which I had experienced in the past but had lost connection with. I needed to show up as love in my life and not expect others to provide me with agape. These were the lessons that it took me more than one relationship to learn. My dear friend reminded me of the effect my learning had on others. He was afraid for me as he watched and I learned through those early relationships.

LOVE WAS INSIDE THE WHOLE TIME

Love expands when we no longer pay attention to the impulse of fear and anger. Instead you begin to cultivate the inner peace of silence. Pay attention to the positive energies in every situation. Love will honor your needs without having to seek outside approval. Believe you're lovable and the pure essence of love just as you are. Seek nothing outside yourself to complete you because you're whole already. You're not broken or in need of fixing. Awaken to the fact that you are what you've been seeking.

PRACTICING BEING LOVE

Look back on your life and see how you've stuck it out. You've done what you needed to do in order to thrive. Look at you: you're adorable, loving, compassionate, creative and all part of the God Head. God created you based on loving thoughts and creativity. You fit into the intricate puzzle of life and you're a unique piece. You're needed and were created for your divine purpose. Look at the essence of you and there God is. Love yourself with the gushy warmth and comfort of the Divine. Practice feeling this way about yourself. Feel the love when you're doing the mundane chores around the house: while you're cleaning house or brushing your teeth feel that love that comforts and gives peace. Rewire your brain so every cell in your body knows what it feels like to be loved from within.

Comfort, security and safety flow through your veins as the loving presence fills you. In each breath you're aware of how much you are loved. You are the love that is you. You have always been loved and adored. Be conscious to the fact that you are the lover and the One who's adored. Can you realize that you're both the giver and receiver of everything? Practice giving this to yourself. Conjure the feeling of this passionate love and carry it with you. When you don't feel it, practice getting it through visioning or ritual.

Practice this technique in your daily life. Know you are loved and imagine that this love is all around you, through you and shows up as you. You are then able to carry this love with you and recognize it in all. You are the embodiment of forgiveness, releasing shame and guilt and letting go of anger and resentment toward others. Don't wait for a reason to forgive. Don't wait for another to apologize to you because your spiritual growth doesn't depend on anyone. Release what has you stuck so the inner Hero is ignited.

AFFIRMATION

I set my identity as having the same attributes of God and because God is Love that is who I AM. I remember that the only option I have during my daily activities is to be loving. My being loving doesn't depend on the circumstance or what another person does; it's based on who I AM.

★ I AM Loving toward myself.

★ I AM Love, because Love is all there is.

★ I AM the seer of all the Love around me.

★ I AM the Creator of Love all around me.

★ I AM the Lover of all creation.

Exercise Ten

Visualize through your spiritual eyes all the love around you. See the beauty and love that you are throughout the day. As you start each day, know that loving thoughts and feelings will be present in every moment ready to share with all you encounter.

Reference

The love we are is best described as Agape, defined as: Love, the highest form of love, especially brotherly love, charity; the love of God for man and of man for God. This love is not based on another person's behavior; it's based on who that person is. We were endowed with the Creator's characteristics and God is Love, therefore that's our identity. We express love as part of our true identity. We see God in everyone, therefore we love them based on who they are not what they've done. This is a higher form of love that's described in the Bless his Heart video.

Video's, "Bless his Heart"& "Love" at drkarmen.com

1 Corinthians 13 New International Version (NIV)

13 If I speak in the tongues of men or of angels, but do not have love, I am only a resounding gong or a clanging cymbal. [2] If I have the gift of prophecy and can fathom all mysteries and all knowledge, and if I have a faith that can move mountains, but do not have love, I am nothing. [3] If I give all I possess to the poor and give over my body to hardship that I may boast, but do not have love, I gain nothing. [4] Love is patient, love is kind. It does not envy, it does not boast, it is not proud. [5] It does not dishonor others, it is not self-seeking, it is not easily angered, it keeps no record of wrongs. [6] Love does not delight in evil but rejoices with the truth. [7] It always protects, always trusts, always hopes, always perseveres. [8] Love never fails. But where there are prophecies, they will cease; where there are tongues, they will be stilled; where there is knowledge, it will pass away. [9] For we know in part and we prophesy in part, [10] but when completeness comes, what is in part disappears. [11] When I was a child, I talked like a child, I thought like a child, I reasoned like a child. When I became a man, I put the ways of childhood behind me.[12] For now we see only a reflection as in a mirror; then we shall see face to face. Now I know in part; then I shall know fully, even as I am fully known.

[13] And now these three remain: faith, hope and love. But the greatest of these is love.

CHAPTER ELEVEN

PRACTICE COMPASSION

*"Chose this day to show compassion, when you hold resentment and unforgiveness.
This is the shortcut on the path to spiritual awakening."*

~ Dr. Karmen

Compassion is activated when we see the suffering of all creation. It's the empathy and love we feel for ourselves when we miss the mark. Only when we give it to ourselves can we share it with everyone else. Compassion is love. Love is all there is and when we feel deep compassion for others we give it to ourselves because there's no separation. Monks when chanting for healing or world peace were asked: "What are you thinking?" "The Oneness of thought is compassion," was the response. When 100 monks are making the unifying OM sound, they all have the intention of compassion.

Compassion is what unifies the shooter and the suicide

bomber with those left with the loss. Compassion is what's employed in the mind of God instead of forgiveness. Forgiveness is what's needed when resentment and anger have formed the ego. Compassion is what's activated through the mind of God. Compassion is what God has for everyone regardless of the act of separation which can take many forms based on The Human Hamster Wheel reactions. But the love and compassion God has for us never changes. When we transform Fear back to Love there's no act that doesn't deserve compassion. When we hold hate and perpetuate suffering we believe there's a lack of love. This is a delusion and can only be overcome through loving.

I realize that when I talk about compassion toward those who are violent or aggressive, some people will have a justification for keeping their anger. There's a Vedic scripture called the *Bhagvad Gita* which translated from Sanskrit means "Song of the Lord". Part of this Hindu text provides a purpose for compassion when Lord Krishna, the possessor of all opulence says, "Fearlessness, pure heartedness, is established in the wisdom of discrimination of spirit and matter by the science of uniting the individual consciousness with the Ultimate Consciousness, charity, self-restraint, performance of sacrifice study of the Vedic scriptures, austerity, uprightness, nonviolence, truthfulness, aversion to fault finding, compassion to all beings, absence of avarice, gentleness, modesty and determination. O Arjuna, radiance, forgiveness, fortitude, purity, freedom from malice, absence of pride; arise in One born of the divine nature." *Bhagvad Gita* 16:1-3

When we discern what's Spirit and what's matter and align with the attributes of God, we can see that all creation is worthy of compassion. When we practice these traits of the Ultimate Consciousness we'll gain more qualities because we've joined with the Creator. When we *dismiss* compassion, peace will not have a vehicle in which to bring forth this outcome. However, when we *affirm* compassion and world peace by showing Love, Gratitude, Acceptance and Trust the light, peace is brought forth through the mind of God.

> *"People pray for world peace but can't hold peace in their heart for two seconds."*
>
> *~ Michael Bernard Beckwith*

AFFIRMATION

I affirm that I AM LOVE. Love is my identifying attribute. Love is all there is because God is all and in all. By affirming who I AM I give myself permission to act and feel from this truth in each moment. This practice can unbind the anger and resentment that can keep the light from shining through us.

- I AM Compassionate toward myself.
- I AM Compassionate toward all of creation.
- I AM Compassionate to all during crisis no matter the act.
- I AM Compassionate regardless of the opinion of the world.

"Getting to know the feel of both emotional energies, fear and courage, will enable you to choose courage more consciously. You don't want fear's energy running rampant in your

beautiful self, even if you know its root. Whenever you're afraid, invoke courage to transform fear, the formula for freedom." ~ Judith Orloff

I would also include Compassion along with Courage in Dr. Judith Orloff's wonderful words of wisdom. It takes courage to express compassion.

Exercise Eleven

Ask yourself the questions: How compassionate are you toward those who've committed violent or aggressive acts? Do you banish them to hell with your judgments? Do you withhold love? Do view them as "the other" creating separation? Write in your I AM journal how you can create wholeness. What would need to happen for you to view people as you view yourself?

Fear is the only thing that can create separation; compassion unites.

Reference

The light when activated by the Five Pointed Star can be the illuminating force in any situation. As a social worker and minister working with families and children in crisis, I've found it very frustrating and stressful if I relied on conventional treatments alone. By connecting on the soul level with hurting people, the interactions aren't stressful and it empowers the therapist and the client toward wholeness. This is the ultimate form of service: to provide an example of wholeness to those who have forgotten their true identity.

"World Peace Prayer" by Ernest Holmes:

"The earth is the Lord's, and the fullness thereof...." I know there is but One Mind, which is the Mind of God, in which all people live and move and have their being.

I know there is a Divine Pattern for humanity and within this Pattern there is infinite harmony and peace, cooperation, unity, and mutual helpfulness.

I know that the mind of man, being one with the Mind of God, shall discover the method, the way, and the means best fitted to permit the flow of Divine Love between individuals and nations.

Thus harmony, peace, cooperation, unity, and mutual helpfulness will be experienced by all.

I know there shall be a free interchange of ideas, of cultures, of spiritual concepts, of ethics, of educational systems, and of scientific discoveries--for all good belongs to all alike.

I know that, because the Divine Mind has created us all, we are bound together in one infinite and perfect unity.

In bringing about World Peace, I know that all people and all nations will remain individual, but unified for the common purpose of promoting peace, happiness, harmony, and prosperity.

I know that deep within every person the Divine Pattern of perfect peace is already implanted.

I now declare that in each person and in leaders of thought everywhere this Divine Pattern moves into action and form, to the end that all nations and all people shall live together in peace, harmony and prosperity forever. So it is--now.

In this video I teach about the process of change. When we embody Love, Compassion, Gratitude, Acceptance and Trust others will be encouraged to awaken to their potential. Video, "How Do People Change?" at drkarmen.com

CHAPTER TWELVE

PRACTICE GRATITUDE

*"I AM grateful for **everything** that happens knowing I have all I need to live my purpose."*
~ Dr. Karmen

Gratitude focuses the mind on life's wonders of which we are one. We're surrounded by beauty everywhere. In the desert we have beautiful sunsets, yet some of us are so busy we don't stop to notice. In *The Color Purple* by Alice Walker the main character says, "God would be insulted if you passed by the color purple and didn't notice it." People may have their head down texting or multitasking, too involved to notice the shape of a tree, the violet in a sunset and a gentle breeze. Notice something and be grateful.

FOCUS YOUR ATTENTION ON GRATITUDE

Deepak Chopra recalled his experience when he was a monk for a month in Thailand. He shaved his head, wore an orange robe and went without his regular comforts. He meditated on his death for hours before dawn and walked barefoot in the streets and forest begging for his daily meal.

He complained to his teacher who was half his age, that his feet hurt. His teacher asked, "Which foot hurts?" Dr. Chopra told him, "The rocks are hurting the bottom of my feet." The teacher responded, "So the one that is on the rocks hurts." "Yes," Dr. Chopra said. The teacher responded, "Both feet are not touching the ground at the same time while you are walking, right?" Dr. Chopra answered, "No." The teacher said, "Put your attention on the foot that is up and not touching the rocks."

This practice of focusing our attention on what's good is a discipline that would serve us well. We create our world based on what we focus on and whatever we focus on will expand. Gratitude is the act of focusing your attention on what serves the highest good. If there's something that doesn't serve the higher good then don't give it your attention. If you practice paying attention to your thoughts, you'd be amazed at how many thoughts you think that don't serve your highest potential.

Our fear-based thoughts consist of judgments, blame, shame and complaints. The ego ruminates over evening the score. It thrives on past pain or future "what if" scenarios. The ego is alive in our thought life which is why we need to be Gratitude Warriors.

BE A GRATITUDE WARRIOR

Being a Gratitude Warrior is a great way to replace the ego's mode of reacting. Gratitude serves us because we're the artists of our future and in each moment we're crafting the next manifestation. When our thoughts are in gratitude we're creating more situations to be thankful for. When we're thankful for the people in our life, we focus our creative powers on increasing the experiences where we can practice love and compassion. Gratitude is the magical colored paint used to create a purpose driven life. While others see the glass as half empty, Gratitude Warriors are thankful for the glass and any amount of water is a blessing.

USING GRATITUDE IN SERVICE.

When I was working as an in-home therapist for the Department of Family Services, I worked with a co-therapist and we teamed up to counsel a single mom and her four children. At our first meeting the co-therapist began asking the mother questions in such a way that put her on the defensive. She became irritated and felt we were passing judgment. As an empath I picked up on her emotional energy and knew she was about to ask both of us to leave even though I hadn't said a word.

So I complimented her on her family pictures that were around the apartment. I told her I was a single mother too and I respected her ability to raise her children without help. I said that many people don't realize how difficult it is to be the disciplinarian, make sure our kids get an education and organize fun things for them to do. I met two of her children and they were so polite that I told her what a good job she had done to raise such courteous children. The client softened and we were able to establish a rapport which helped in the therapeutic process.

The co-therapist told me I was one of the most positive people he had ever met. I didn't see it necessarily as being positive; I saw it as practicing gratitude in order to manifest more of her strengths. The family came into the system because of a lack of protection; I didn't want to focus on the problem which caused her to be defensive. Being defensive is a common reaction when accused of something. I didn't want to instigate shame, anger or guilt in the client because those emotions perpetuate suffering. Instead I focused on being grateful for her children because I know that from that light comes lasting change.

IGNITE THE INNER HERO

To have lasting change I needed to focus on what was working so I could ignite her inner Hero. I acknowledged her strengths and the good things she was doing with her family despite the difficulties. By focusing my attention on her strengths she was able to feel appreciated and empowered so she could discuss the parenting skills she needed guidance in. She was doing her best at the time and we needed to acknowledge that fact. Everyone is doing their best at any given moment based on their level of consciousness. By using gratitude as a therapeutic tool, the mom could replace "I am a bad mom" with "I am all I need to keep my kids safe and well". This is the place where she wants to be and I just needed to see her that way. Seeing something before it's manifested allows miracles to come forth.

What I learned from being a clinician is that feelings of guilt and shame perpetuate the cycle of suffering. Only when we empower another to look within can they replace the victim mentality that manifested the behaviors in the first place. The mother needed to work with someone who could see past the current behaviors that led to the abuse and neglect charges to who she truly was. When she heard her strengths through another person's words, she believed she could do better. When people believe their value and worth, they see the worth of the negative situation which allowed the realization of this truth.

REMINDER

My job as a clinician is to remind people of who they are. I believe all those in the helping professions should know who they are before they begin working with clients. Through self-realization we can serve as a reminder for others. If we don't know who we are and are not grateful for our journey, then how can we help others who are stuck on The Human Hamster Wheel?

Being grateful for the journey is more important than reaching the destination. When we're grateful for all that's happened in our life, we reach a spiritual precipice. We see how everything's been working together for our highest good all along. Viewing our life from this vantage point allows us to transcend the thoughts of regret or victimization; we now see with eyes of understanding and wisdom. We can see how relationships failed or loss occurred to bring us to a deeper realization of our identity. We become less judgmental of others and their behavior because it's all part of their journey to Self.

PRACTICING GRATITUDE

I saw a commercial on television advertising orange juice and immediately received a deeper truth. I incorporate this way of viewing circumstances into my daily practice. In the commercial the woman is sitting at a table with all the mishaps she's going to encounter later that day. There's a mechanic and a teacher, to name a few. The tow truck driver tells her she parked in the wrong place and he'll be towing her car. She says, "Great, and when I chase after you yelling 'Stop' you keep going?" He says, "Yep." She says, "Fabulous." Her professor tells her she'll have to sprint across campus to get to class and she'll still be late. She's overjoyed and says, "At least I'm starting the day with my orange juice." The tow truck driver says, "Just not your car."

The deeper meaning I gleaned from this commercial was how we let circumstances and situations steal our joy. The woman attributes her joy and good mood to orange juice but we have the power of the Universe working for our good no matter the circumstances. I adopted this way of looking at situations for a period of a year. So for one year, no matter what happened, I would be elated about it, knowing that no matter what, God had my back. I was advised at work that I had a flat tire soon after I declared this as a practice. People thought I was smoking crack. They didn't understand how seemingly bad news could elicit a smile and a shout of "Yes!"

I admit this may have looked wacko but I wasn't concerned about how it would look to others. I was rewiring my brain to see all things as good. I had no problem seeing a flower as good or an unexpected check in the mail as a fantastic thing. I needed help seeing "ALL" things as working together for my ultimate good. I discovered I could change my whole energy toward any situation. I was guarding against having the victim mentality resurface. Igniting the inner Hero begins with gratitude. When we practice gratitude we become aware of our thoughts and feelings which either create the victim or ignite the hero.

COMPLAINING BUDDIES

When I started the practice of being thankful for everything, I noticed I had to call an end to my complaining buddies. These are people I cultivated in my life who were there so I could vent about how bad things were. I was in a relationship with someone who collected all the negative things in their day to inform me of them when I got home. At the start of the day we would talk about everything negative that would probably happen. We would anticipate the bad. My complaining buddies were essential in my life and the conversation was my ego's way of coping with my perceived victimization. My ego felt charged by complaining, criticizing and blaming.

So I cultivated these types of relationships. I was casting these characters based on my need to have comrades to agree with my victimhood. I picked them out of central casting because I AM in control of my reality. Therefore I take full responsibility for the characters who show up. I AM so powerful that I can choose not to be a victim. When thoughts are filled with blame, it takes the power of transformation out of your hands. Your inner Hero awaits.

We can all make a million excuses and justifications for our behavior and that's why it can be difficult to change. The benefit I drew from those complaining sessions was to draw power from talking negatively about people or situations. I created separation between myself and the one I was criticizing, feeling superior in the process. I would argue my opinion about something and demean someone who I perceived did something wrong to me. All those sessions gave me power fueled by a job and a life where I identified myself as a victim.

I could continue to deny that these complaining buddies were detrimental to my spiritual growth but once I decided who I AM and began to practice forgiveness, gratitude and compassion I could no longer participate in complaining. Igniting the hero within stopped the judgmental impulse which was my way off The Human Hamster Wheel.

CHANGING THE CAST OF CHARACTERS

In my close relationships I began a practice of telling the other person all the good that happened that day. My partner at that time was stumped; it was as if he had to find different regions of his brain to understand my "foreign" language. We had to learn to be consciously thankful in our conversations. We had hardwired our brains to look for negative things throughout our day to talk about. Now we had to train ourselves to look for positive things or evidence of the truth which is "All things are working together for good".

When I met with my complaining buddies, I tried to introduce consciously creative ideas into the conversation. They would look at me like I had five heads. I was the main instigator of the bitch sessions for years and had habitually complained to gain some sense of power and control by portraying myself as the victim. When I practiced gratitude and tapped into my inner Hero, I was throwing a wrench into our group. As I introduced positive and creative ideas to facilitate growth and empowerment, the group disbanded. There was no longer a role for me to play so the group broke up on its own.

By being the I AM and igniting my inner Hero, relationships I'd formed while on The Human Hamster Wheel began to evaporate or change form. My connection between my inner Hero and others changed significantly. I could no longer participate in the sport that I drew energy from. I would listen to my coworkers complain and smile. I would grin from ear to ear because of an inner knowing of what they were really saying. They were stuck and afraid not knowing how to see the world without making their suffering someone else's fault. This is a survival response built at the lowest frequency of fear. I smiled because the Universe was teaching us how to get off the Hamster Wheel and ignite our inner Hero. The Universe was constantly showing us what needed to be shifted and transformed within us.

When gratitude is a daily or even hourly practice the old ways of getting power externally feel awkward and unsatisfying. If I were to criticize now as I did then, I would hear myself and wonder who that impostor was. Who said that? Where did that come from? I AM consciously aware when I slip up and make a comment from my old ego. I quickly self-correct by briefly assessing my trigger, showing compassion toward my actions and in the next moment I AM grateful for the opportunity to practice.

PRACTICE GRATITUDE

Remember the orange juice commercial? No matter what happens, recognize that the Universe is working together with you for your highest good. Suffering is a birthing of the greater self in disguise. Be in gratitude with over-the-top elation. This practice can rewire your brain and change the way you view suffering. I certainly don't see suffering or trauma in the same way I once did and I can truly say I'm thankful for everything that's happened in my life. Not just the good stuff but everything because it's made me more of who I AM. These experiences help me to share on a deeper level and develop channels of understanding that increase my level of service. I couldn't write this book without them.

A GRATITUDE JOURNAL

Keeping a gratitude journal is a good practice. Writing down all you're grateful for during the day can rewire your brain. A special journal dedicated to everything you're grateful for can be a way to bring forth more good into your material life.

Teaching children to do this helps them be grateful for their life experiences and they'll be able to see the blessings in everything. A ritual of sharing their gratitude journal with the family once a week or monthly will develop a stronger bond. By sharing at the dinner table each blessed event of the day your family will create connections through positive energy instead of the typical complaining, stressful energy.

AFFIRMATION

By affirming we're grateful for our life we unkink the victim viewpoint. The truth is we're not victims. To change the paradigm of victimization we replace complaining and blaming with gratitude.

> ✭ *I AM Grateful for everything in my life.*
> ✭ *I AM Grateful for the attributes of acceptance, love, trust and compassion.*
> ✭ *I AM Grateful for my pure vision which allows me to focus on the good.*
> ✭ *I AM Grateful for the positive loving vibration that's real.*
> ✭ *I AM Grateful for the intention of God which is to give.*
> ✭ *I AM Grateful and trust that the Universe is rigged in my favor.*
> ✭ *I AM Grateful that I accept more good in my life.*
> ✭ *I AM Grateful for my past and my present.*

"And we know that for those who love God all things work together for good, for those who are called according to his purpose." Romans 8:28

Exercise Twelve

At every red light pick one thing you're grateful for before the light changes. This is a wonderful practice that incorporate gratitude in your daily activities, the more you practice, it will become as natural as breathing. Your breath becomes the ultimate prayer for being thankful for everything in life.

Reference

When we're grateful for all our experiences, we chip away at the victim mentality. We receive the mind of the Creator.

In this video I give an example of being grateful during a lecture at University of Nevada Las Vegas.
Video, "1 Minute Reminder: Being Grateful for Everything" at drkarmen.com

CHAPTER THIRTEEN

PRACTICE ACCEPTANCE

"By God, when you see your beauty you will be the idol of yourself."
~ Rumi

I had a relative who told me about an experience she had when she was depressed and confused. She had signed up for a meditation class and during her silence she felt the love God had for her. The inner voice she heard in her spirit conveyed: "If you only knew how much I love you". She felt a love come over her that she couldn't contain. She began to cry and said the feeling was indescribable. She felt loved beyond words. I advised her to practice that feeling daily so she could carry it around with her. Her inner voice had said to her, "If only you knew", meaning there was something within her that had been blocking this ever present feeling of being loved. By practicing this feeling with affirmations or thoughts she could accept the truth. Acceptance is essential in expressing and knowing the mind of God.

A few weeks had passed since her initial experience when I connected with her again. She told me she had been on the subway when she noticed an Asian girl who had a unique style from her hair and glasses to her tights and tennis shoes. She thought to herself: Look at how GOD has decided to show up today. The girl's style symbolized how creative God is. She was also touched by how joyful it was to recognize GOD's creation. She said she looked around the train and saw God's presence in everyone. She cried at the beauty and magnificence when looking through the eyes of the Universe. She was grateful for the privilege to see behind the veil with her spiritual eyes. When we can view the material world through the lens of God we can see things as they truly are... miraculous.

The truth of her experience will reverberate through her everyday life. When we Accept that the presence of God is everywhere and there's no place where God is not, we open ourselves to experience miracles of divine sight. These soulful experiences have the ability to redefine our identity giving us access to the creative and powerful vision in each moment. We all have the ability to see the creation and hear that loving voice within. This woman was given the opportunity to divinely be what she experienced. She accepted this love within and as a result was able to accept everyone else as loving beings. She shined her light and thus saw everyone on the subway with the heightened level of consciousness.

Many people have experienced this form of joyful revelation of love, including my son. He was driving and listening to his favorite inspirational song when he said the consciousness of love began to resonate in his soul. He had heard this song for more than a year but this time it became intertwined with his soul. He began to cry uncontrollably as a warm feeling of love washed through him. He was love in that moment. He had to pull over to the side of the road to allow this presence within to reveal itself.

I advised my son to accept that this love was coming from within him and not an outside entity. It's important to recognize that love, creativity and power are within us and not to be found outside our consciousness. Within us is the Divine. Without the blockages we put up we're free to accept our true nature.

ACCEPT WHAT HAPPENS BY CHANGING YOUR PERCEPTION

One of the most awesome manifestations of joy came three years after I lost my dream home to foreclosure during the recession. I grieved that loss yet knew I had to let it go so I could learn the lessons it was there to teach. Over the next three years I aligned with the attributes of God by forgiving myself and accepting my fiancé whom I had tried to change. All my fiancé did was reveal my fear-based insecurities. I realized I needed to let go of the belief that someone was supposed to save me. That relationship made me realize that I AM the savior, a role I had previously assigned to my fiancé. This was a big miracle for me to accept that I'd been looking outside myself for my security. Many of my biggest trials were designed to wake me up to the fact that I AM all I need. This BIG revelation broke a cycle of suffering that had taken generations to learn. I now accept all my experiences because they bring me to myself.

> *"We have been given the creative power to manifest using love energy. Our thoughts and feelings are energy that we use to create our physical world."*
> ~ Dr. Karmen

MANIFESTING THE DESIRES OF YOUR HEART

I practiced the Five Pointed Star and reconnected with the power within me. As a result of my inner change my outer reality also morphed. I was able to buy a house that was the exact same model as the house that went into foreclosure, only better. This was such a manifested miracle that I still freak out walking around my house now. I not only bought my dream house but did it without the need of a bank. The house represented proof positive that God was working to show me what's possible when I release fear and stop blaming everybody.

My insecurity and powerlessness had a strong hold in my life and when I accepted full responsibility for my healing everything changed. When I became aware of my fears and stepped out using love instead, the I AM took over. The I AM or inner Hero manifested something that was so much bigger than I could comprehend and that's when I knew reclaiming my identity creates miracles. Miracles were showing up in my life and I couldn't intellectually describe my experiences. When I tried to articulate my miraculous manifestation, people wanted to make my home a logical consequence of planning. There was nothing logical about it. Every bit of it was a manifested miracle which was beyond words I could articulate therefore beyond explanation. I remember getting blank stares and comments that weren't associated with what I was conveying. I vowed to tell only those who had an intention for and acceptance of the miraculous.

People would ask me if I saved to buy the same model house back. I would say, "No". The truth was I began to manifest miracles when I cultivated the qualities within myself that I was seeking out in the world. Through culture and the way I was raised I believed a man was going to save me financially. I thought in order to get what I wanted I needed to have a man. On a surface level I would have said no way, I don't believe that; however my actions told a different story. If I was insecure about money, the answer was a man. If I was feeling unattractive, the answer was a man to affirm me. If I felt stupid, then I wanted a man to tell me I was smart. This could be traced directly to my childhood experiences with my parents and the disconnect to who and what I truly AM. My mother taught me to rely on a man to provide happiness and fulfill my needs. When the man doesn't perform these duties and live up to our expectations then we have him to blame. Having someone to blame provides built-in denial and perpetuates the cycle of suffering.

ACCEPT YOUR PURPOSE

You don't have to be on television or write a *New York Times* best seller in order to be a spiritual teacher. I began to step into my purposeful life of service with those within my circle of existence: a coworker, my son and myself. A coworker I didn't know became the target of my divine service. Whenever I was with this coworker my inner Christ voice would tell me that God loved him. I felt the intensity of love toward that person and it was overwhelming. After several palpable experiences of this, I went up to him and told him, "God wants me to tell you that he just loves you so much". My coworker didn't know what to do with this information but thanked me and went on his way. I felt the need to do this each time I saw him and by the third time we sat down and talked. I didn't really know this gentleman but I wanted clarification as to why I was overcome with such agape love for him.

He told me he was spending many hours at the hospital with his six-year-old son who had been sick for a long time. His child was born with a disease that was causing his health to decline. He stated his wife and church family were actively in prayer. A couple of weeks later I was in my office and got a strong inner message to go to the hospital. As I was driving I was advised by this same inner voice to stop by the bank and withdraw $1,000. I put the money in an envelope and went to the hospital. There in the ICU waiting room was my coworker and his family. He told me his son had just died. I was shocked as I assumed I was going there to give words of encouragement. Instead I gave him and his wife a hug and handed them the envelope as I left. I was confused and didn't know why I came.

When I got back to the office my phone rang and my coworker said that when I walked into the hospital waiting room he and his wife were wondering how they were going to bury their son. They opened the envelope I gave him and saw the $1,000 and it was an answer to their prayer. He asked how

I knew to go to the hospital. All I could say was that I learned to trust and accept that when I connected with the mind of God there was nothing keeping me from the action that followed. I listened to the still small voice inside me and I showed up as God for someone who believed in miracles.

ACCEPTING THE VESSEL EXPERIENCE

When experiencing Oneness with the Universe, the mission is to be in service to Spirit. That Spirit is within me, you and all beings. When I open myself up to Spirit then I'll be serving its purpose through me. This is the vessel experience. The source of all fills you up so you can be of service to others. Through this cycle miracles are manifested. The "I AM" Solution experience is being available to expose the highest potential in everyone and every experience you encounter. Really all you're doing is revealing or reminding people of who they are. Being empowered to give like the Creator is the ultimate vessel experience. The "I AM" Solution is about being in service to the One.

While in the zone of the vessel experience, I was conducting workshops in the Juvenile Detention girls unit every Saturday morning. About 35 girls would attend the workshop. I used the movie *The Matrix* to teach them about their true self-worth. The movie provided a wonderful metaphor of our inner Hero connection to something bigger. It's a sci-fi classic and has deep spiritual concepts that can be used to reclaim our true identity. Every Saturday I would let the girls in the unit know that they are the One and within them is all the power and love they'll ever need.

One particular Saturday my inner Christ voice told me to tell the person in the back row, third to the left that she is loved. What came over me was a gushy overwhelming feeling of Divine Love. I was toward the end of the lecture and instead of complying with my inner knowing, I wanted to leave and get on with the rest of my day. All that week the nagging feeling was there. I needed to tell that girl that she's loved. I was hoping she would be in detention the next week because if not, I would have to track her down. I was anxiously awaiting my lecture in detention that Saturday because finally I could do what I was asked to do and give her the message. Saturday came and there she was.

At the end of the workshop I asked her if we could talk privately. I told her, "Last week God told me to tell you you're loved and that he loves you so much it's more than you could believe. I was supposed to tell you last week but I wasn't being obedient and I'm so glad I get a chance to tell you now how much you're loved." The girl broke down and cried saying she had gotten caught up in prostitution and did things she was ashamed of. She had been asking God over and over, "Do you still love me?" She told God to give her a sign and she hadn't gotten one until now. I told her there was nothing she could do that could make God stop loving her. I said, "He loves you because he is love and his love is not based on your behavior; it's based on who you are. You and God are One and are not separated by anything but your thoughts."

BEING THE ONE

Being is when we cultivate and "accept" within ourselves everything we're looking for outside. Then all that's attached to those attributes will materialize in our life. I was insecure and my relationship with my fiancé didn't fix it. I still felt vulnerable, unsafe, unimportant and underappreciated. I began to understand that it wasn't about my fiancé but about me already being important, safe, confident and appreciated. Once I understood that I was what I was looking for, miracles showed up without pushing, manipulating or being anxious about it. My ego was no longer in the driver's seat. I was being what I was looking for. I was being what I thought the other person should have provided. As soon as I made this paradigm shift, I no longer needed to blame, manipulate and criticize because the truth set me free from The Human Hamster Wheel.

Instead of being angry with my fiancé for not providing what I wanted (which would have been my Hamster Wheel paradigm) I loved him for exactly who he was *without judgment*. The agape love I showed him was part of the tools of manifesting the miracle. If I would have left the relationship with anger and hatred I would not have been able to experience abundance. If I would have blamed him for all my troubles then I would have continued on The Human Hamster Wheel of suffering, creating more of the same.

When I first felt the shock of the pending implosion of my relationship and the stresses of my job filled with conflict, my declining health and my son cutting me out of his life, I knew the Universe was trying to tell me something. I needed to figure out how to stop repeating chaotic drama. I needed to get back on the spiritual path. I needed to stop the emotional reactions that kept reverberating from my past. I needed to love and accept the people around me. I had to forgive others and myself. I had to show compassion and stop trying to change others but trust that they're on their right path. I focused on forgiving, loving, having compassion, being non-judgmental and having gratitude. When I practiced these attributes my inner guide or spiritual GPS turned on and began directing my actions. In the past my emotions guided me. As an empath, these emotions could easily be coming from another person so I couldn't let my erratic moods lead me anymore. The acceptance practice allowed me to accept and recognize that some emotions aren't my own and I don't need to act on them but be aware of them. Acceptance is one of my main daily practices.

AFFIRMATION

Acceptance of the love, power, beauty and the talents we have is key to sharing them with the world. When we doubt, fear and diminish the wonder of who we are, we can't be of service. When we accept and acknowledge who we are, and that God is within us, we make room for more light or as they say in *Star Wars*: "May the Force be with you".

★ *I Accept that it's time to move on when something no longer serves my higher purpose.*
★ *I Accept that there may be a different path.*
★ *I Accept and release the need to control and to struggle.*
★ *I Accept that my value is not determined by other people.*
★ *I Accept that I AM divinely made.*
★ *I Accept that my power is not determined by manipulation or control.*
★ *I Accept that there's a lesson in everything.*

> ★ *I Accept that it's not my job to fix another person.*
> ★ *I Accept that fear is a delusion.*
> ★ *I Accept that love is all there is.*
> ★ *I Accept that I AM a powerful Creator.*
> ★ *I Accept that I AM the attributes of God.*
> ★ *I Accept that I AM limitless.*
> ★ *I Accept that based on my inner consciousness I can change my outer reality.*

CONSCIOUS CREATIVITY

There's something exciting about having the desire to seek the Kingdom or mind of God. The Kingdom of God is the consciousness of infinite possibilities where anything is possible. In quantum physics this consciousness could be called a parallel Universe, which to me means that at any given time there are infinite realities going on simultaneously. Set your intention for the highest consciousness to access the universal abundance which has already been provided. All you need to do is match its intentional vibration. In this moment be the One to access the abundance. Can you accept this truth?

ACCEPTING AND TRUSTING THE I AM

Visioning is a practice that can support the truth of parallel universes. Envision the highest intention for yourself and others. In your vision be as specific as possible. I AM seeing with the vibrational energy what already exists. See within or envision as if the experience is happening now. When you match the feeling (excitement, butterflies, etc.) as if it's happening now you're bringing forth what the feeling is connected to. The brain believes it's real when you feel the emotion that came with your vision. For example, I imagined myself with my own office and being a therapist long before I finished college. I went to a uniform store when I was in community college and bought a white doctor's coat. I had my name Dr. Smith embroidered on the right side. I wore it around the house and knew it would happen one day. I had a prop and was elated by my accomplishment years before it was manifested.

My cousin is an author and she had a vision board she looked at it every time she turned on the computer. She had Oprah's book club on the screen which is a dream of most authors. A year after being published she was sitting across from Oprah talking about her book. Visioning does work whether it's a vision board, a prop or sitting quietly while you feel and see your future. It really does work! We are more than we realize. God is in us and we are in God. Keep in mind that your vision already exists and you're bringing it forth because the abundance is here and now.

This visualization coupled with the feeling that comes with the reality causes the path to show up at your feet. You're using your energies to create the now. In the past the ego used most of our energy to fight with the past and manipulate the future. Being is when we consciously create the path that's representative of our highest self or our inner Hero. The path is there already; all we have to do is bring it into being.

*"In the creation of any form it is necessary for its image to exist in Mind
before it can come into realization in the external."*
~ Ernest Holmes, Author of *Science of Mind*

VISUALIZATION

Accept that you are the majesty of the Grand Canyon, the beauty in the orchid, the freedom in the butterfly and the compassion in the child. You are all of that and it may take a lifetime to comprehend the complex simplicity of your identity but it's a worthy lesson. Usually this knowledge of who we are comes from suffering but when the material world loses its hold over our identity, our inner Hero is allowed to guide us.

INNER HERO

The experience of being brings joy. I AM a joyful being in the presence of the Divine Spirit which is all around me. I AM grateful for being in the presence of the Love, Compassion, Forgiveness, Power, Abundance and Creativity that is me.

Exercise Thirteen

In this exercise ask: Who do I think I AM? Because whatever you think your identity is will determine how you show up in the world. The hurting people who have a concept of victimization will show up as abusers or victims. In order to be a victor you must see yourself in an empowering light. In your I AM journal write down what's going on right now in your life and see if you're a victim or a victimizer—or a victor!

Reference

"Who are you?" is a primary question because it will determine your lot in life. How do you answer this question? This video uses some pictures from a trip to the holy land to ask the question: Who are you? See if you agree with the answer and write the response in your I AM journal.
Video, "Who are YOU?"

In the next video is an inspiring quote by Marianne Williamson from her book, *A Return To Love:* Reflections on the Principles of A Course in Miracles, recited by my sister Kimberly Ann Harris.
Video, "Our Deepest Fear" both at drkarmen.com

CHAPTER FOURTEEN

PRACTICE TRUST

> *"And you can break yourself free from your hereditary patterns, cultural codes, social beliefs; and prove once and for all that the power within you is greater than the power that's in the world."*
> ~ Michael Bernard Beckwith

When I'm working with a client, I need to trust that both of us will get something positive out of the experience. Being a parent, I need to trust that my son will make good decisions. Any anxiety or worry is a sign that I don't trust the source within. My first and lasting reaction to someone who's stuck on The Human Hamster Wheel is compassion. The next response I have is to trust. I trust they'll have the insight needed to transform their inner world so it's reflected in the outer one. Everything we experience in the material world is a reflection of our inner thoughts and beliefs. Therefore when we or someone we encounter is suffering, based on their outside circumstances, I affirm that they'll gain the insight to ignite their inner Hero. It may not happen—in their lifetime or mine but it will happen. The earth is a classroom and we may have many opportunities to learn but our ego hinders us from fully engaging in the transformation process. The process will take place but when and how may be beyond our knowledge. Yet we must trust it will happen at some point.

The soul is eternal and I trust there will be an ignition toward enlightenment. I don't need to know when and I don't need to know how. I may not see the end of anyone's suffering but I will treat them and see them as though healing is now. I AM grateful for the ability to see through the mind of GOD or the inner Hero's vision. This inner vision allows us to see through the lens of the architect. When we trust in this process, we affirm it through our words and thoughts. When our thoughts are aligned with the love energy of God we can see God everywhere. In the most hurting people we can see their inner Hero even when they're blind to it themselves.

What's important is that we know when we're not ourselves: when we feel awkward and out of character. When we know a slip up has happened and we weren't aligned with the intention of God, it's important that we don't beat ourselves up. The shame that may come from our harsh self-criticism puts us right back on The Human Hamster Wheel. Be the loving teacher for yourself that you are with others. These slip ups or sins are a signal of a lack of love and your fear triggers will be activated and can bring up the old paradigm of suffering. The triggers continually remind us that we need to return to the love. We need to be awake and practice the points on the Five Pointed Star which when activated in our life will center us within the mind of God. Reclaim, reconnect and take a deep breath, confident in who you are. Be grateful for the instructional experience and move forward to the next moment. Trust that you're everything you need and everything is working for your good.

THE BLACK MADONNA AND THE BIRTHING OF THE CHRIST CONSCIOUSNESS

I've been fascinated with the Black Madonna for years and have a picture in my home of her holding Jesus. When I went to Europe, I saw the Black Madonna icon in the churches and shops. I stared at and took pictures of the figures not understanding the meaning or significance. In the United States these icons aren't displayed. I was raised in the African Methodist Episcopal (AME) Church and there was little mention of Mary and no images of her in the sanctuary. So I was mesmerized by the Black Madonnas I saw when I traveled to Greece and Italy. The Catholic churches in Europe were ornate with statues and pictures of Mary. I later learned that the Black Madonna came from an African Goddess who was depicted as a Black woman pregnant with a snake. The snake symbolizes birth and regeneration.

Ancient wisdom teaching refers to the Black Madonna as the force that continually loves us and wants us to come into the Christ Consciousness and know our true identity. The Black Madonna wants to birth in us the inner Hero, this Christ consciousness. Her presence lets us know that as we go through the painful birthing process we're not alone. The mother is the awesome feminine partner of the masculine which makes up the Divine presence and brings opportunities for growth. The Black Madonna is the answer to the dualistic thought of suffering. Instead of the dualism of good and evil, we can defy our fearful thoughts and enter into God's thoughts in all situations.

Both male and female energies define the process of creation. We might mistake the birthing pains for the absence of God's loving presence but the intention behind the event is to bring forth Oneness with the Source. In the Hindu religion Shiva is the God of destruction and rebirth and is not to be feared but acknowledged. When we interpret suffering or change as bad, it will determine our path. Therefore we need to redefine such tearing down or change as part of the process of becoming One with the Source. Humans can interpret suffering through the lens of a victim from a limited fear-based perspective or view it as divine expansion. The Black Madonna and Shiva are pulling the ego apart in order to restore our TRUE SELF. The light is released in us as we're broken open by the events in The Human Hamster Wheel of Suffering. When we trust this process as symbolized by Mother Mary, we can ease into transformation knowing we're part of a loving act.

TRUSTING THAT SUFFERING IS THE PROCESS OF BEING

The Kingdom of God transcends suffering by connecting us to our TRUE SELF. The suffering is always a call to come home. The Black Madonna represents everything on The Human

Hamster Wheel of Suffering, however to wake up, we must see the truth behind the trauma—which is that at any point the "birthing" can take place. Through labor pains the loving consciousness can be restored in us. The Black Madonna brings forth the Christ Consciousness within us and will continue to give more revelations of the loving Spirit we were created to be.

The Divine Mother trusts that all beings will come to the realization of who they are. The Black Madonna knows that the purpose of all events is to be interpreted based on a birthing of a deeper understanding of Self. Loving intentions of transformation are the Black Madonna's motivation.

How do we align with the whole of ourselves? While on the Hamster Wheel we feel broken, shameful, victimized and less than who we are. We may feel alone in our pain but it's the birthing or reawakening of the Christ Consciousness that brings the end of the perception of suffering. The Christ Consciousness transcends the perception of loss and violation into Love, Compassion, Acceptance and Trust. These attributes allow the suffering to be a loving teacher, which is the intention of the feminine Godhead.

"We are not broken and don't need fixing"
Panash Desai, Author of Your Soul's Signature

TO BE OF SERVICE IS WHY WE SHOULD TRUST THE PROCESS OF TRANSFORMATION

Service is the ultimate goal of Oneness. When we go through the dark night of the soul and gain wisdom of the true Self we can show others the way. The hero's journey is realized when we overcome our fear and are able to teach others who need to be reminded of their identity. Coming to the knowledge through suffering is the loving work of the Madonna, Shiva, Ego and Satan (blockage). Whatever name you call it or how you conceptualize the challenge the goal is for higher consciousness. The vehicle that brings us to the truth is not to be cursed but to be trusted in order to transport our perceptions from the delusional state. The Divine Spirit that's in all is in the service of giving and requires our whole identity. The perception of lack or brokenness will only serve to perpetuate darkness or chaos.

SERVICE

There are no better drug counselors than those who used to have a drug dependency. Those who have been through the struggle of suffering can best show the way to the other side. It's still that individual person's journey to take but the example of wholeness is healing. Jesus gave an excellent example of wholeness to the disciples. The 12 were able to watch him as he confronted injustice, healed the sick and as the saying goes "walked the talk". When people see the way we handle stress or challenges that strengthen rather than cripple us, they gain insight into who they are. Jesus said, *"I AM the way and the truth and the life. No one comes to the Father except through me. If you really know me, you will know my Father as well. From now on, you do know him and have seen him."* John 14:6

He was explaining the Christ consciousness or way of thinking which allowed him to live his life according to the mind of God. In other words the way I have been living is based on the thoughts that are aligned with God, therefore if you see how I live you see the Father who sent me. I AM not only representing him but you can't tell the difference because we are the same, creating from the same attributes and my intentions come from God. Now that you know how I AM you can Be the Father. Jesus said, "If you really know me..." meaning those who have the Christ consciousness of God recognize it in him.

Examples are very important for learning any skill or talent. In math class I needed many examples before I could understand how to solve the problem on my own. The calculus teacher would write the equation on the chalkboard and then go step by step in order to teach the class how to solve it. Several examples were included in the book for each complex equation. The answers were in the back of the book but our teacher didn't want us to write just the answers; we had to show the way we solved the problem. All of the great sages, teachers and prophets showed the way to live a more loving life. When they developed the Christ consciousness, by returning to love it showed up as a life of service to the Creator.

When you are of service trust that your story is a balm to others and that nothing is wasted. No matter how ugly, shaming or painful, your story has a healing ingredient once you're empowered by it. Remember, with the Christ Consciousness nothing is broken and the world needs to see the example of Wholeness.

"The ultimate measure of a man is not where he stands in moments of comfort and convenience, but where he stands at times of challenge and controversy."
~ Dr. Martin Luther King, Jr.

BEING IN THE ZONE

Several years ago I was in the zone of being my authentic Self. What I experienced was a connection to God that was miraculous and through me I was serving in a way that manifested miracles. I remember being in the moment and having been told audibly what to do and what to say to another person. At first I was hesitant and concerned about what others would say. I was curious about this presence within that was loving and generous. I was new to the experience of being One with God and was still skeptical, yet I knew I was experiencing a new way of being.

When working with juveniles in detention almost 20 years ago, I looked into their faces and saw space and stars. That's right—instead of a nose and eyes I would see a vision of the cosmos briefly and then I would see their face. I saw the cosmic nature of humans. I was given this vision of who they really are because I was connected to the Christ Consciousness. I saw how magnificent these teens were who had stolen cars, assaulted people and cursed at staff. They were not in the disguise of the flesh but were bigger than their behaviors. I saw the stars when I looked into their faces—the colors, textures and deeper light that was within. I saw the magnificent presences of the Divine and it was all around me moving at different speeds and intensities. I AM blessed to have glimpsed this energy of the Universe in EVERYONE. I can appreciate and have a knowing of what is there even though I haven't experienced that intensity since. I experienced that wonder of a moment because I was seeing this truth within myself.

AFFIRMATION

When we trust the process of change and the Creator, we release the fears that used to paralyze us. As we see our outer world reflecting more of our inner consciousness we know everything is going to work out. As our mind aligns with our Creator we see the effects of peace, love and abundance in our life.

☆ *I Trust that I AM loving, compassionate, grateful and accepting.*
☆ *I Trust that I AM healed.*
☆ *I Trust that I AM not healed alone.*
☆ *I Trust that I AM given opportunities to express my true self.*
☆ *I Trust that everything is working together for good.*
☆ *I Trust that the Universe is rigged in my favor.*
☆ *I Trust that I AM the mind of God made flesh.*
☆ *I Trust that I AM used for the service of God.*
☆ *I Trust that I AM the source of all things.*
☆ *I Trust that I AM all there is.*
☆ *I Trust that I AM all I need.*

According to certain tribes, the *Sacred Space* is the space between exhalation and inhalation. To *Walk in Balance* is to have Heaven (spirituality) and Earth (physicality) in harmony. At the core of this timeless wisdom is the word "trust". When did we stop trusting ourselves? When did we start giving that trust, that *power*, away? In many ways the Spirit path is a process of reestablishing that trust with the infinite that resides within us, just waiting to be activated.

LAKOTA PRAYER

Great Mystery,
teach me how to trust
my heart,
my mind,
my intuition,
my inner knowing,
the senses of my body,
the blessings of my spirit.
Teach me to trust these things
so that I may enter my Sacred Space
and love beyond my fear,
and thus Walk in Balance
with the passing of each glorious Sun.

Exercise Fourteen

In this practice pay attention when your mind begins to worry about something. In your I AM journal, write down ways you could be an example of wholeness. Those within your circle are looking at your actions and words to see if you're walking the talk. Are you consistently practicing the Five Pointed Star to align you with the thoughts of God? Practice not concerning yourself with the outcome of a situation; instead know and trust everything is going to be okay. Let go of the need to know how everything will work out; trust and affirm all things are working together for good. People are reaching their highest level of consciousness and they don't need fixing; they need an example of wholeness. When people ask you about a challenge, you can repeat your affirmation with conviction trusting a good outcome. Don't give energy to doubt, fear, worry or conflict. This way of trusting takes practice.

Reference

In the book *The 72 Names of God, The Technology for the Soul*[TM] by Yehuda Berg, the names are codes that when scanned regularly can rid one of depression, stress, anxiety and physical ailments. These names can be included in your daily practice by scanning the Hebrew letters from right to left. In the video I show the Hebrew letters and discuss their sacred significance. Set your identity at the beginning of the day; don't take on the world's definition of you.
Video, "72 Names of GOD"

In the next video I share my daily practice and remind you to align with your true identity. Your practice can be anything you choose that puts you in a more loving, non-judgmental and trusting intention. In this video I'll show you how you can combine Qi Gong movements with imagery to customize your daily practice.
Video, "The 'I AM' Solution Practice" both at drkarmen.com

CHAPTER FIFTEEN

THE "I AM" SOLUTION

"Darkness cannot drive out darkness; only light can do that.
Hate cannot drive out hate; only love can do that."
~ Dr. Martin Luther King, Jr.

The "I AM" Solution begins with the desire to have lasting love in your life. Not romantic love but the love that allows you to share without fear of rejection or loss. Once you determine that you want to live a life without fear the answers are found inside your thoughts. When you have a desire to eliminate the drama by getting to the root of the fear-based thinking that's kept you stuck, then The "I AM" Solution provides answers.

The EGO or as I call it The Human Hamster Wheel of Suffering, seeks power and control when our fear leads to anger, shame and guilt. These emotions are developed when our hurt goes unrecognized by compassion. As a result of our experience caused by the lack of compassion, our true identity (love) is transformed to fear. FEAR stands for: From Ego Altering Reality. When we live our lives based on our fears we see the world through the lens of our pain. We view people and the world based on what we project upon them. Therefore when we react in fear and blame others, we're reacting based on an altered reality. Fear creates the delusion of separation from love. Fear distorts the world and makes it impossible to see the truth which is that God is all there is. Love is the manifestation of the consciousness of God which is all creation. While we live in fear we're looking in a fun house mirror thinking the distortions are real.

Embody the transcendent."
~ Dalai Lama

The good news is that when we finally recognize we're creating our chaos, then we can transform the Fear back to Love. The Five Pointed Star is a practice to help align you with the love source within you. Affirming the love that you are can be a powerful practice toward eliminating self-hatred. The critical voice from the ego begins to dissipate as you recognize your true identity. Shame and guilt can't find a home within a loving temple. Be Love.

By affirming Compassion we'll never have to forgive again. God doesn't forgive because there's compassion when we miss the mark. When we've already judged, the anger that we felt and the resentment that we stored has to be released, through forgiveness. When we're walking with compassion and love there's no need to forgive. When people are hurting, upset, struggling and showing all the behaviors on The Human Hamster Wheel, Be Compassion.

By affirming Gratitude, we become thankful for the experiences that helped us step into our higher consciousness. The "so called" negative experiences we now recognize as the catalyst for positive change. Being grateful daily opens our consciousness up for more good to come. When we appreciate the little things, we're acknowledging the big things that are on the way. Gratitude is a weapon against the victim mentality because you can't be grateful and complain at the same time. In Genesis, after God completed a project like creating the earth and the oceans, there was time to admire and appreciate the creation. Always appreciate everything that's in creation. Be Grateful.

By affirming Acceptance, we give up the need to know all the answers. We accept that the consciousness that guides us has the plan, blueprint and GPS. We need to release control and be guided by our purpose. We can accept people wherever they are and whoever they are as a part of the One. Acceptance allows us to view people the way God sees them—without the judgments that separate us. In order to view the world the way God sees it which is our goal, stereotypes, traditional loyalties and racism no longer serve us. We accept the magnificence that we are. We are beautiful, powerful sources of divine energy. We accept that we have gifts and talents that are given by the Creator. We accept that we are made in the image of God. Be Accepting.

By affirming Trust, we know that by attaining the mind of God we embody the I AM. Trust and knowing surpass belief and enable us to be more empowered in our life. If I AM in a classroom and I say to the teacher I *know* something, it's more powerful than if I say I *believe* it. When we trust our spiritual process and the Creator, we leave doubt behind and step out into the unknown, knowing it's divinely guided. Trust is when you know everything is working for your good. Trust is not being influenced by fear because you know the Creator is providing the knowledge and direction. Many times I've been called to speak without a script but I know the Creator within me will form the words. I don't have to worry; I just have to trust. Be Trusting.

When you practice the Five Pointed Star on a daily basis opportunities will arise in your life to shine the light. Your presence will be different and therefore those around you may have an experience of light. Remember you deliver the light, so don't be concerned about the outcome. Your only contract is between you and the Creator, not the person you share the light with.

Trust that the light will do the work and all we have to do is turn on the light within ourselves. We must trust that the process of activating our connection to the light is for a bigger purpose which may be beyond our vision. We can't rely on our five senses to convey or make sense of our journey. Our purpose and bliss will be revealed by an inner thought, sensation or experience that confirms our existence. Be of Service

When we release the need to control and surrender to the energy presence within, all that's there is JOY. Void of struggle, fear and doubt, JOY is the natural result of igniting the hero within. Joy can be seen in children because they have no screen. Most children experience their feelings without the fear of being judged. Children enter a room of toys and they're elated and naturally curious about the items that catch their eye. They want to touch, grab, pull, push and hold everything to get the essence of that object. As they discover this wonderland, their elation is contagious. They're so excited that they want to know what's next. When in this state they enjoy each moment.

As you know by now I'm a movie buff and this joyful state reminds of the original *Willy Wonka and the Chocolate Factory*. The 1971 movie has many deep spiritual concepts like the Wizard of Oz. The chocolate factory owner sends out five golden tickets in his candy bars. Millions of people try to open as many candy bars as they can in order to get the golden ticket and win a chance to tour the factory which has been closed for decades. When the five lucky winners enter the big wonderland where everything is magical and edible the music starts. The kids and adults dart in every direction in joy and wonder at the magical candyland. Willy Wonka sings the song, Pure Imagination, which explains how our thoughts create reality.

PURE IMAGINATION

Hold your breath
Make a wish
Count to three

Come with me
And you'll be
In a world of
Pure imagination
Take a look
And you'll see
Into your imagination

We'll begin
With a spin
Traveling in
The world of my creation
What we'll see
Will defy
Explanation

If you want to view paradise
Simply look around and view it
Anything you want to, do it
Wanta change the world?
There's nothing
To it

There is no
Life I know

To compare with
Pure imagination
Living there
You'll be free
If you truly wish to be

If you want to view paradise
Simply look around and view it
Anything you want to, do it
Wanta change the world?
There's nothing
To it

There is no
Life I know
To compare with
Pure imagination
Living there
You'll be free
If you truly
Wish to be

    I never get tired of that scene because I know the Universe whispers to us the importance of imagination. Every time we view a situation through the lens of the doubters that block our creativity, a still small voice beckons us to return to the mind of God...pure imagination.

    When we practice the Five Pointed Star we can have wonder and curiosity and our view of the world will reflect our inner state of joy and wonder.

⭐ *Love yourself and all creation.*

⭐ *Be Grateful for each moment and breath.*

⭐ *Show Compassion toward yourself and others.*

⭐ *Accept that this world is a magical place and you are a magician.*

⭐ *Trust that God made you to Be the One.*

Joy is the byproduct of practicing the Five Pointed Star. Joy won't be found in outer experiences but within like a bubbling well—it's reliable and never runs dry. This Joy is contagious and your coworkers and family will wonder what you're smoking. Just tell them it's The "I AM" Solution™.

"The More you are motivated by Love the more fearless and free your actions will be."
Dalai Lama

Exercise Fifteen

Contemplate the following passage from *Living the Science of Mind*. Trust and know that this is the truth. Let go of any prior learning that's not in alignment with this truth. Write your thoughts in the "I AM" journal.

"Not only is there a Presence within us which directly responds to us; there is also a Law operating through us which obeys the will of the Presence. Since this Presence is Peace, Joy, and Beauty, and since It must be Harmony and Wholeness, we may be sure that these qualities seek expression through our activities, seek manifestation in everything that we do, say, and think...The Life within you is God; whatever is true of God is true of your life, since your life and the life of God are not two but ONE."
~ Ernest Holmes, Author of *Living the Science of Mind*

Reference

When we practice the Five Pointed Star our light is activated. We are ready to be of service. When we are of service to the light we are the delivery system. Our contract is between us and the Creator. When we understand our purpose, there's no pressure to fix another person or situation because the light does the work.
In this video I describe this process of delivering the Light, so you can be of service to the Creator.
Video, "Delivering the Light" at drkarmen.com

A copy of the poem "I AM There" is on the moon, carried on Apollo 15 by astronaut James B. Irwin. It was left there for future space voyagers.

I AM THERE
by James Dillet Freeman

Do you need me?
I Am there.
You cannot see me, yet I Am the light you see by.
You cannot hear me, yet I speak through your voice.
You cannot feel me, yet I Am the power at work in your hands.
I Am at work, though you do not understand My ways.
I Am at work, though you do not recognize My works.
I Am not strange visions. I Am not mysteries.
Only in absolute stillness, beyond self, can you know me as I Am, and then but as a feeling and a faith.
Yet I Am there. Yet I hear. Yet I answer.
When you need Me, I Am there.
Even if you deny Me, I Am there.
Even when you feel most alone, I Am there.
Even in your fears, I Am there.
Even in your pain, I Am there.
I Am there when you pray and when you do not pray.
I Am in you and you are in Me.

The "I AM" Solution

Only in your mind can you feel separate from Me, for only in your mind are the mists of "yours" and "mine."
Yet only in your mind can you know Me and experience Me. Empty your heart of empty fears.
When you get yourself out of the way, I Am there.
You can of yourself do nothing, but I can do all.
I Am in all.
Though you may not see the good, good is there, I Am there.
I Am there because I have to be, because I Am.
Only in Me does the world have meaning; only out of Me does the world take form; only because of Me does the world go forward.
I Am the law on which the movement of the stars and the growth of living cells are founded.
I Am the love that is the law's fulfilling.
I Am assurance. I Am peace. I Am Oneness.
I Am the law that you can live by.
I Am the love that you can cling to.
I Am your assurance. I am your peace.
I Am One with you.
I Am. Though you fail to find me, I do not fail you.
Though your faith in Me is unsure, My faith in you never wavers, because I know you, because I love you.
Beloved, I Am there.

ABOUT THE AUTHOR

Dr. Karmen Smith is a Licensed Clinical Social Worker and an ordained Minister (Doctor of Divinity). In college her major was Mental Health Research with an emphasis on learning and processing information and a minor in Human Biology. Her Masters is in Social Work.

Dr. Karmen has over 20 years' experience working in the Child Welfare and Mental Health fields. She's discovered a strong link between psychological principles and spiritual beliefs and their ability to change behavior. She's helped many people stop their abuse cycle and live drama free lives.

Dr. Karmen had pain that she carried around for years which poisoned other aspects of her life. She had grown up in a home with domestic violence, sexual abuse, physical abuse and alcoholism. She hated her father for most of her life calling him her Sperm Donor. She felt resentment and anger and wanted revenge against the wrongs she felt he had done. These feelings seeped into her relationships and her work environment, and her weight was out of control. She was unaware of the painful experiences she was creating with her emotions.

One day she had a miraculous life-changing event that allowed her to forgive her father and release the pain she had carried from every cell in her body. Not only did her relationships improve but her finances improved as well. After this experience she wanted to find a way to teach what she'd learned. She wanted it to be easy to understand and implement so anyone could use it to change their lives.

From that miraculous experience Dr. Karmen developed a unique approach with techniques and practices in a program used to forgive oneself and others and release the pain to live a forgiving life. What she believes is you no longer need to hold onto hate, and that unforgiveness can have an impact on health causing stress and creating experiences of trauma.

Dr. Karmen's intention is to offer her years of experience by helping clients release the pain of trauma and fear. She found that people who suffered from painful experiences held onto the trauma and it showed up in every aspect of their life. They created addictive experiences such as alcohol or drug abuse, toxic relationships, poor health or generational poverty.

By using the techniques of forgiveness that are as ancient as the Bible, Dr. Karmen developed THE "I AM" SOLUTION which anyone can implement to get amazing results. Everything that shows up in our lives is directly related to who we believe we are. The path to changing the world begins from the inside out. Through the process of forgiveness and connecting with the consciousness of God you can change the way you see the world by transforming Fear back to Love.

CONTACT INFORMATION

Dr. Karmen Smith, MSW LCSW DD
Karlcsw@gmail.com
www.DrKarmen.com
Facebook: https://www.facebook.com/TheIAMSOLUTION
Twitter: @drkarmensmith
Sign up for the Online Course The "I AM" SOLUTION ™

The Five Pointed Star

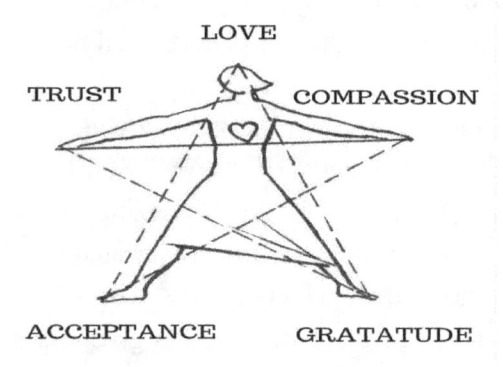

LOVE
TRUST
COMPASSION
ACCEPTANCE
GRATATUDE

SHINE YOUR LIGHT ~ PEACE AND BLESSINGS

CPSIA information can be obtained
at www.ICGtesting.com
Printed in the USA
BVHW04s2152211018
530851BV00016B/144/P

9 780997 120509